ACCA
Taxation (TX – UK) FA 2018

First edition 2007, Thirteenth edition October 2018

ISBN 9781 5097 2295 2

e ISBN 9781 5097 2296 9

British Library Cataloguing-in-Publication Data

A catalogue record for this book is available from the British Library

Published by

BPP Learning Media Ltd
BPP House, Aldine Place
142–144 Uxbridge Road
London W12 8AA

www.bpp.com/learningmedia

Printed in the United Kingdom

Welcome to BPP Learning Media's ACCA **Passcards** for **Taxation (TX – UK)**.

- They **focus on your exam** and **save you time**.

- They incorporate **diagrams** to kick start your memory.

- They follow the overall **structure** of the BPP Study Texts, but BPP's ACCA **Passcards** are not just a condensed book. Each card has been separately designed for clear presentation. Topics are self contained and can be grasped visually.

- ACCA **Passcards** are still **just the right size** for pockets, briefcases and bags.

Run through the complete set of **Passcards** as often as you can during your final revision period. The day before the exam, try to go through the **Passcards** again! You will then be well on your way to passing your exams.

Good luck!

For reference to the Bibliography of the Taxation (TX – UK) Passcards please go to:
www.bpp.com/learning-media/about/bibliographies

		Page			Page
1	Introduction to the UK tax system	1	11	Partnerships and limited liability partnerships	65
2	Computing taxable income and the income tax liability	9	12	National insurance contributions	69
3	Employment income	23	13	Computing chargeable gains	73
4	Taxable and exempt benefits. The PAYE system	27	14	Chattels and the principal private residence exemption	81
5	Pensions	35	15	Business reliefs	87
6	Property income	41	16	Shares and securities	93
7	Computing trading income	45	17	Self-assessment and payment of tax by individuals	97
8	Capital allowances	51	18	Inheritance tax: scope and transfers of value	105
9	Assessable trading income	57	19	Computing taxable total profits and the corporation tax liability	115
10	Trading losses	61			

		Page			**Page**
20	Chargeable gains for companies	123	23	Self-assessment and payment of tax by companies	139
21	Losses	131	24	An introduction to VAT	143
22	Groups	135	25	Further aspects of VAT	153

Contents

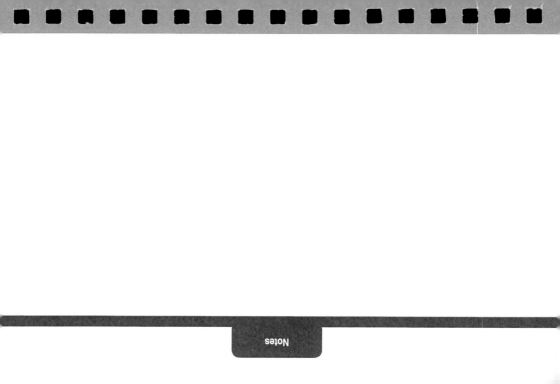

Notes

1: Introduction to the UK tax system

Topic List

The overall function and purpose of taxation in a modern economy

Different types of taxes

Principal sources of revenue law and practice

Tax avoidance and tax evasion

This chapter contains background knowledge which underpins the whole of your later studies of taxation.

Economic factors

Taxation represents a withdrawal from the UK economy. Tax policies can be used to encourage and discourage certain types of activity.

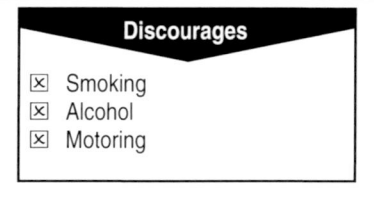

Encourages
- ☑ Saving
- ☑ Charitable donations
- ☑ Entrepreneurs
- ☑ Investment in plant and machinery

Discourages
- ☒ Smoking
- ☒ Alcohol
- ☒ Motoring

Social factors

Tax policies can be used to redistribute wealth:

- Direct taxes – tax only those who have these resources
- Indirect taxes – discourage spending
- Progressive taxes – target those who can afford to pay

Environmental factors

Taxes may be levied for environmental reasons:

- Climate change levy
- Landfill tax

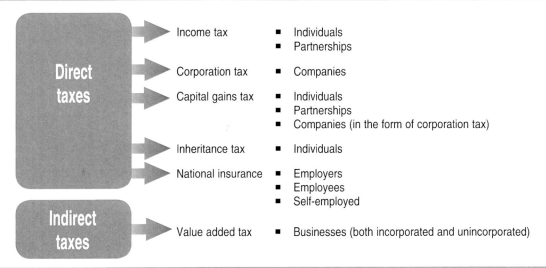

Direct taxes	Income tax	<ul><li>Individuals</li><li>Partnerships</li></ul>
	Corporation tax	<ul><li>Companies</li></ul>
	Capital gains tax	<ul><li>Individuals</li><li>Partnerships</li><li>Companies (in the form of corporation tax)</li></ul>
	Inheritance tax	<ul><li>Individuals</li></ul>
	National insurance	<ul><li>Employers</li><li>Employees</li><li>Self-employed</li></ul>
Indirect taxes	Value added tax	<ul><li>Businesses (both incorporated and unincorporated)</li></ul>

Structure of the UK Tax system

Treasury

⬇

HM Revenue and Customs ➡

- Officers of Revenue and Customs
- Crown Prosecution Service

Appeals heard by:

- First Tier Tribunal (most cases)
- Upper Tribunal (complex cases)

Sources of revenue law and practice

Law
Statute
Statutory instrument

Practice
Statements of practice
Extra-statutory concessions
Explanatory leaflets
Revenue and Customs Brief
Internal Guidance (HMRC manuals)
Agent Update

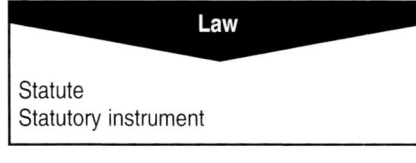

European Union

- States may agree to enact Directives to provide for common taxation
- Value added tax (VAT) Directives oblige UK to pass laws in accordance with EU legislation
- Tax provisions which discriminate against EU freedoms may be ineffective due to treaty direct effect
- Exchange of information

Double taxation agreements

- Prevents income or gains being taxed in more than one country
- Income/gain taxed in one country only or credit given for tax in one country against tax in other country
- Non-discrimination provisions to protect foreign nationals
- Exchange of information

Tax evasion

Tax evasion consists of seeking to mislead HMRC by either:

- Suppressing information, or
- Providing deliberately false information.

Illegal

Tax avoidance

Tax avoidance includes any legal method of reducing your tax burden, eg:

- Using tax shelters, or
- Participating in schemes designed to minimise tax.

Legal

General Anti-Abuse Rule (GAAR)

- HMRC can counteract tax advantages from abusive tax arrangements.

- Tax arrangements involve obtaining a tax advantage as (one of) their main purpose(s).

- Arrangements are abusive if they cannot be regarded as a reasonable course of action **and** result in eg significantly less income, profits or gains being taxable.

- Tax advantage includes relief or repayment of tax.

- HMRC may counteract tax advantages arising by eg increasing the taxpayer's tax liability.

Concerns whether client is honest with HMRC

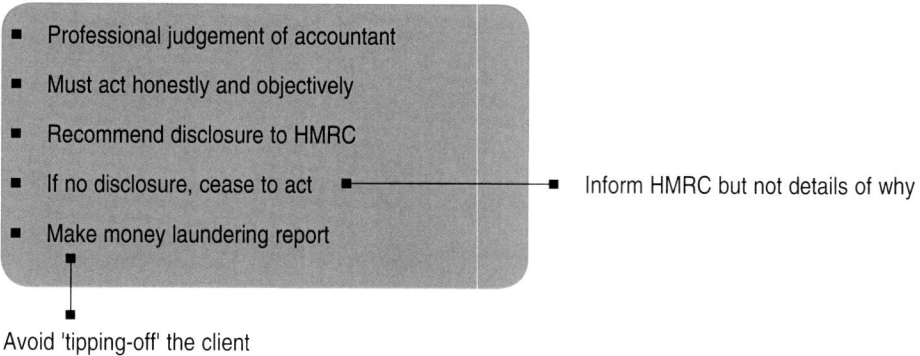

- Professional judgement of accountant
- Must act honestly and objectively
- Recommend disclosure to HMRC
- If no disclosure, cease to act ■ ———— ■ Inform HMRC but not details of why
- Make money laundering report
■

Avoid 'tipping-off' the client

2: Computing taxable income and the income tax liability

Topic List

Scope of income tax

Computing taxable income

Chargeable/Exempt income

Qualifying interest

Computing income tax

Accrued income scheme

Gift aid

Child benefit income tax charge

Transferable personal allowance

Married couples/civil partners

The computation of income tax is a key exam topic. One of the 15 mark questions in Section C will focus on income tax. Income tax will also be tested in Section A and may also appear in the 10 mark questions in Section B. This chapter deals with computing taxable income which draws together all of the taxpayer's income. You will also see how the income tax liability is computed on taxable income. We also look at the accrued income scheme on gilts, how gift aid donations are given tax relief, the computation of the child benefit charge, the transferable personal allowance between spouses/civil partners and how jointly held property is taxed.

An individual who is UK resident is taxable on world-wide income.

Test 1st: Automatically not UK resident

- In UK < 16 days in tax year

- In UK < 46 days in tax year, not resident in any of three previous tax years

- Works full time overseas throughout tax year, not in UK > 90 days in tax year

Test 2nd: Automatically UK resident

- In UK ≥ 183 days in tax year
- Only home in UK
- Works full time in UK in tax year

Test 3rd: UK ties

Number of ties required
to be UK resident
depends on number of days
spent in UK in tax year
(see Tax Tables)

- Close family (spouse or civil partner/minor child) resident in UK
- Home available in UK, used in tax year
- Substantive work in UK
- In UK > 90 days in either of two previous tax years
- Spends more time in UK than anywhere else in tax year (if previously resident only)

Aggregation of income

A basic principle of income tax is the **aggregation of income**. All of an individual's income for a tax year is added up in a personal tax computation as **total income**.

Net income

Total income minus qualifying interest and trade losses.

Adjusted net income

Net income less grossed up gift aid/personal pension contributions.

Taxable income

Net income minus personal allowance.

Tax liability

The amount of tax charged on income.

Tax payable

The balance of the tax liability still to be paid.

Personal allowance

£11,850 for 2018/19

Restrict if adjusted
net income > £100,000
by £1 for each £2 excess
(nil if ≥ £123,700).

Types of income

The main types of income for individuals are:

- Profits of trades, professions and vocations

- Income from employment and pensions

- Property income

- Savings and investment income, including interest and dividends

Exempt income ■——■ Leave exempt income out of personal tax computations.

- Premium bond prizes
- Income from Individual Savings Accounts (ISAs)
- Returns on National Savings Certificates

Qualifying interest

Interest paid on a particular type of loan is deducted from total income to compute net income.

- For purchase of an interest in a partnership
- For purchase of plant and machinery for partnership (purchase must be by partner)
- For purchase of plant and machinery for use in employment (purchase must be by employee)

Computing income tax

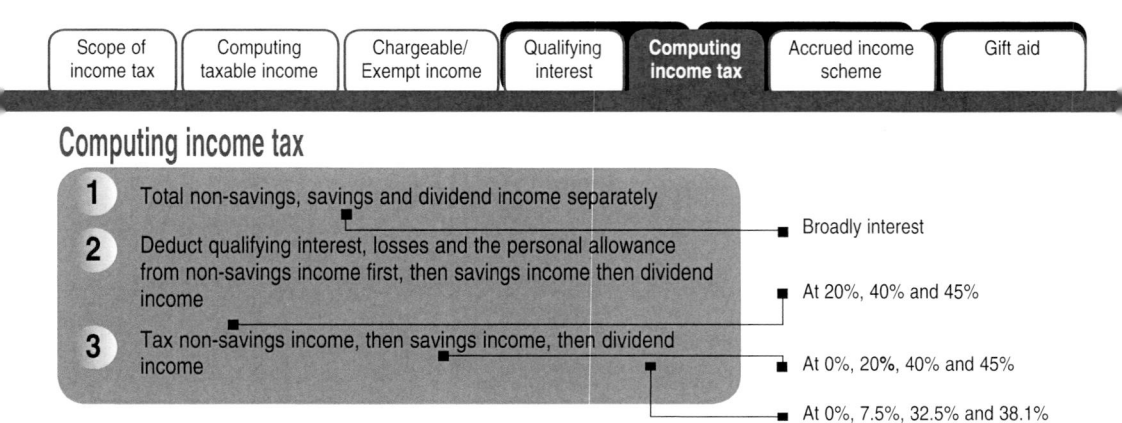

1 Total non-savings, savings and dividend income separately

■ Broadly interest

2 Deduct qualifying interest, losses and the personal allowance from non-savings income first, then savings income then dividend income

■ At 20%, 40% and 45%

3 Tax non-savings income, then savings income, then dividend income

■ At 0%, 20%, 40% and 45%

■ At 0%, 7.5%, 32.5% and 38.1%

There is only one set of rate bands to cover all types of income.

The basic rate limit and higher rate limit must be increased by the gross amount of any gift aid donation/personal pension contribution (amount paid × 100/80).

If non-savings income does not exceed the starting rate limit, then the savings income is taxed at the starting rate 0% up to the starting rate limit (£5,000). Also taxed at 0% in savings income nil rate band (£1,000 basic rate taxpayer, £500 higher rate taxpayer). £2,000 dividend nil rate band for all taxpayers.

Accrued income scheme

- Applies on sales of government securities (gilts).
- If sold with right to next interest payment:
  - Seller taxed on accrued interest in proceeds as savings income
  - Purchaser given relief for accrued interest in proceeds against interest actually received
- If sold excluding right to next interest payment:
  - Seller given relief for accrued interest in proceeds against interest actually received
  - Purchaser taxed on accrued interest in proceeds as savings income

Example

Julius owned £12,000 (nominal value) 3% gilts. Interest paid 30 June and 31 December each year. Julius received interest of $6/12 \times £12,000 \times 3\% =$ £180 on 30 June. Sold to Wynona on 30 September with right to next interest payment. Proceeds included accrued interest to 30 September of $3/12 \times £12,000 \times 3\% = £90$. Wynona received interest of $6/12 \times £12,000 \times 3\% = £180$ on 31 December.

Julius: taxed on £(180 + 90) = £270 savings income

Wynona: taxed on £(180 − 90) = £90 savings income

Gift aid

- Gift aid donations are charitable gifts of money which qualify for tax relief.
- Donor must make a gift aid declaration to the charity.

Basic rate

Basic rate tax relief given by treating donation as net of basic rate tax

Higher and additional rate

Higher and additional rate tax relief given by increasing limits by grossed up donation

Child benefit charge

- Child benefit is paid to individual who cares for at least one child
- Usually paid to mother and exempt from tax
- Charge reclaims child benefit received by taxpayer or partner

Adjusted net income > £50,000 < £60,000

Charge is 1% of the child benefit amount for each £100 of adjusted net income in excess of £50,000

Adjusted net income ≥ £60,000

Charge is full amount of child benefit received

Transferable personal allowance

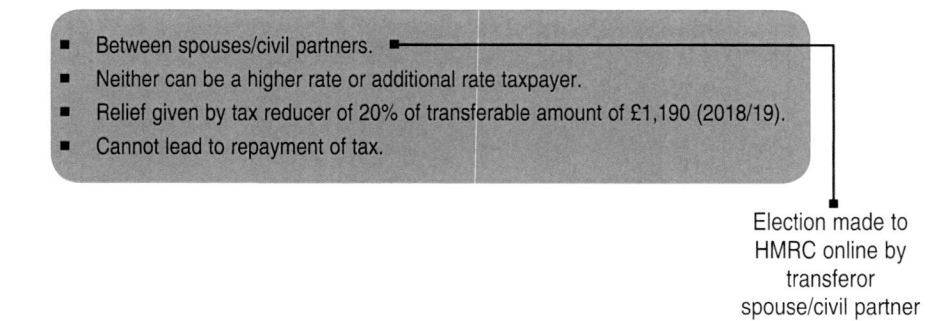

- Between spouses/civil partners.
- Neither can be a higher rate or additional rate taxpayer.
- Relief given by tax reducer of 20% of transferable amount of £1,190 (2018/19).
- Cannot lead to repayment of tax.

Election made to HMRC online by transferor spouse/civil partner

Jointly held property

Spouses and civil partners often hold property jointly, sometimes in unequal proportions.

For tax purposes treat the income received from such property as shared equally.

If the actual interests in the property are unequal, spouses/civil partners can declare this to HMRC and income is then shared in actual proportions.

2: Computation of taxable income and the income tax liability

Tax planning for married couples/civil partners

- Consider transferring assets to ensure that both spouses/civil partners use savings income nil rate bands and dividend nil rate bands.

- Then consider transferring assets to spouse/civil partner with lower marginal tax rate.

Example

Tim and Lucy are a married couple. Tim is a basic rate taxpayer (savings nil rate band £1,000) and Lucy is a higher rate taxpayer (savings income nil rate band £500). Tim has savings income of £1,500 but no dividend income. Lucy has dividend income of £4,000 but no savings income.

Tim should transfer funds generating £500 interest to Lucy so she uses her savings income nil rate band.

Lucy should transfer shares generating £2,000 dividends to Tim so he uses his dividend nil rate band of £2,000.

3: Employment income

Topic List

Employment and self-employment

Basis of assessment

Allowable deductions

Although this exam is mainly computational you may be asked to describe the difference between employment and self-employment in a Section C question.

You also need to be aware of the final two topics in this chapter: when employment income is assessed and the deductions that you may be able to make in computing the amount of assessable employment income.

Employed or self-employed

An employee works under a contract of service and a self-employed person under a contract for services.

Whether a contract is a contract of service or a contract for services will depend on a number of factors.

Factors

- The degree of control exercised over the person doing the work
- Whether they must accept further work
- Whether the other party must provide further work
- Whether they provide their own equipment
- Whether entitled to benefits eg pension
- Whether they hire their own helpers
- What degree of financial risk they take
- What degree of responsibility for investment and management they have
- Whether they can profit from sound management
- Whether they can work when they choose
- The wording used in any agreement between parties

Employment income

Employees/directors are taxed on income from the employment:

- Cash earnings
- Benefits

↓

Earnings are taxed in the year in which they are received.

The general definition of the date of receipt is the earlier of:

- The time payment is made
- The time entitlement to payment arises

→

Directors are deemed to receive earnings on the earliest of the following:

- The time given by the general rule
- The time the amount is credited in the company's accounting records
- The end of the company's period of account (if the amount has been determined by then)
- When the amount is determined (if after the end of the company's period of account)

The general rule is that expenses can only be deducted from earnings if they are incurred wholly, exclusively and necessarily in performing the duties of the employment.

- The strictness of this test has been emphasised in many cases.

Expenses specifically deductible against earnings:

1 **Insurance** premiums to cover directors' and employees' liabilities (and payments to meet those liabilities)

2 **Subscriptions** to relevant professional bodies

3 **Qualifying travel expenses** – costs the employee incurs travelling in the performance of their duties or/and travelling to or from a place attended in the performance of duties

4 **Contributions** (within limits) to a registered occupational pension scheme

5 **Payments to charity** under a payroll deduction scheme

- Normal commuting does not qualify.
- Relief is available for expenses incurred by an employee working at a temporary location on a secondment of 24 months or less.
- If a mileage allowance is paid relief is available for any shortfall of allowance actually paid below statutory mileage allowance.

Exam focus

If you have to decide whether an expense is deductible, put yourself in HMRC's position and try to find an argument against deducting it. If you can find a specific argument, the expense is probably not deductible.

4: Taxable and exempt benefits. The PAYE system

Topic List

Taxable benefits

Exempt benefits

The PAYE system

Benefits may be tested as part of a Section C question or in Section A or B, so it is vital that you are able to calculate the taxable value of benefits provided to employees. You also need to be aware of the benefits that are exempt from tax.

The deduction of tax from employment income through the PAYE system is also important.

General business expenses

Automatic exemption for reimbursement if expense would be allowable deduction for employee.

Vouchers

- Cash vouchers
- Credit token
- Non-cash vouchers

Taxable benefit is cost of provision.

Accommodation

Annual value of accommodation is a taxable benefit, unless job related.

Additional charge if costs more than £75,000.

Original cost plus the cost of improvements incurred prior to start of tax year

Excess multiplied by official rate of interest at the start of the tax year

Living expenses

Living expenses connected with accommodation (eg gas bills) are taxable. However, if the accommodation is job-related, the maximum amount taxable is 10% of net earnings.

Vans

- £3,350 charge if available for private use (not home/work commuting)
- £633 charge for private fuel

Page 29

4: Taxable and exempt benefits. The PAYE system

Loans

1. Loans of over £10,000 give rise to taxable benefits equal to the difference between the actual interest and interest at the official rate.

2. A write-off of a loan gives rise to a taxable benefit equal to the amount written off.

Cars

Annual taxable benefit for the private use of a car is (price of car – capital contributions) × % related to CO_2 emissions:

- Cars emitting 0–50g/km = 13%
- Cars emitting 51–75g/km = 16%
- Cars emitting 76–94g/km = 19%
- Cars emitting 95g/km = 20%. Percentage increases by 1% for each 5g/km (rounded down) up to 37%.
- Percentage increased by 4% for diesel engined cars (not above max 37%).
- Benefit scaled down on a time basis, if car not available all year.
- Benefit then reduced by any contribution by employee for private use.
- Fuel for private use is charged as percentage of base figure £23,400, 2018/19. Same percentage as car benefit. No reduction for partial reimbursement by the employee.

Private use of asset

In general, if an asset is made available for private use, the annual taxable benefit is 20% of the market value when the asset was first provided, less any employee contribution.

If the asset is subsequently given to the employee the taxable benefit is the higher of:

(i) Original MV less amounts already taxed

(ii) Market value at date of gift less any employee contribution.

■ Not used if asset is bicycle

Other benefits

■ Taxable value of other benefits charged on employees.

■ Cost of provision of benefit less any employee contribution

Exempt benefits

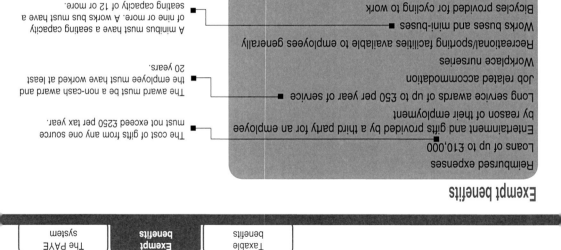

- Reimbursed expenses
- Loans of up to £10,000
- Entertainment and gifts provided by a third party for an employee by reason of their employment
  - The cost of gifts from any one source must not exceed £250 per tax year.
- Long service awards of up to £50 per year of service
  - The award must be a non-cash award and the employee must have worked at least 20 years.
- Job related accommodation
- Workplace nurseries
- Recreational/sporting facilities available to employees generally
- Works buses and mini-buses
  - A minibus must have a seating capacity of nine or more. A works bus must have a seating capacity of 12 or more.
- Bicycles provided for cycling to work
- Parking places at or near work

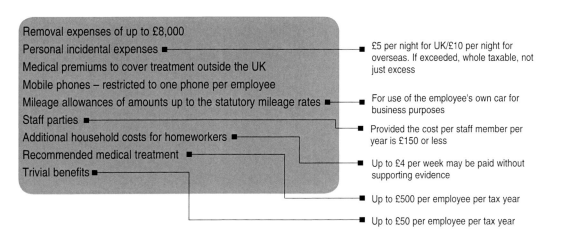

Removal expenses of up to £8,000

Personal incidental expenses — £5 per night for UK/£10 per night for overseas. If exceeded, whole taxable, not just excess

Medical premiums to cover treatment outside the UK

Mobile phones – restricted to one phone per employee

Mileage allowances of amounts up to the statutory mileage rates — For use of the employee's own car for business purposes

Staff parties — Provided the cost per staff member per year is £150 or less

Additional household costs for homeworkers — Up to £4 per week may be paid without supporting evidence

Recommended medical treatment — Up to £500 per employee per tax year

Trivial benefits — Up to £50 per employee per tax year

The PAYE system collects tax from employees each payday, with the intention that over a tax year, the correct total of tax due will be collected.

How PAYE works

- Employer makes FPS to HMRC electronically on or before date of payment ('Real Time Information')
- Includes details of amounts paid to employees, income tax and national insurance deducted, starting and leaving employees
- Calculations made using PAYE codes, usually on cumulative basis
- Employer can choose to payroll benefits instead of reporting on P11D

Payment

The employer must pay over the tax and NIC deducted up to the 5th of each month by the 22nd of that month if electronic payment (19th if by cheque). Penalties for late payment (except first).

PAYE code numbers

- L: Code with personal allowance
- M: Code if receiving £1,190 of personal allowance from spouse/civil partner
- N: Code if giving £1,190 of personal allowance to spouse/civil partner

PAYE settlement agreements

PAYE settlement agreements are arrangements under which employers settle employees' income tax liabilities on certain benefits and expense payments.

Forms

Form P60 – to employee by 31 May
Forms P11D – to HMRC and employee by 6 July
Form P45 – to employee when leaves employment

5: Pensions

Topic List

Types of pension scheme

Contributions to pension schemes

Receiving benefits from pension arrangements

A single regime applies to all pensions, whether occupational or personal.

Pension contributions are a tax efficient way of saving for retirement.

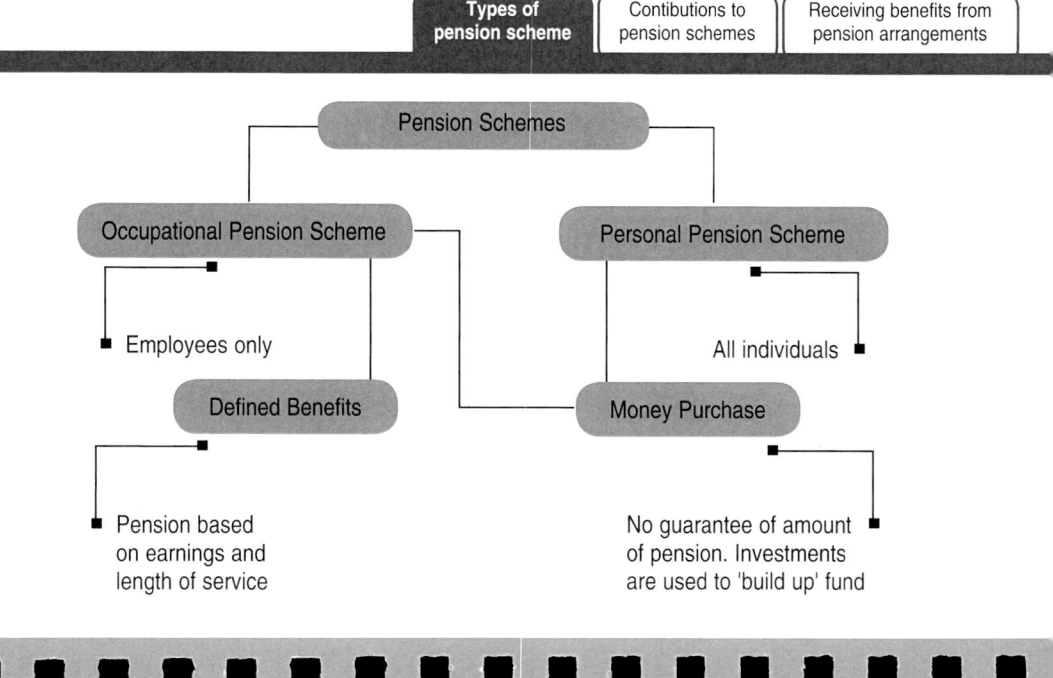

Pension Schemes

Occupational Pension Scheme

Personal Pension Scheme

■ Employees only

All individuals ■

Defined Benefits

Money Purchase

■ Pension based on earnings and length of service

No guarantee of amount ■ of pension. Investments are used to 'build up' fund

Annual limit

Maximum contribution attracting tax relief is higher of:

- Relevant earnings
- £3,600 pa

Lifetime allowance

£1,030,000 is maximum value for pension fund.

- Employment income, trading income and furnished holiday lettings income

Employer contributions

- Count towards allowances (annual and lifetime)
- Trade deduction for employer
- Tax free benefit for employee
- No NIC for employer or employee

Annual Allowance

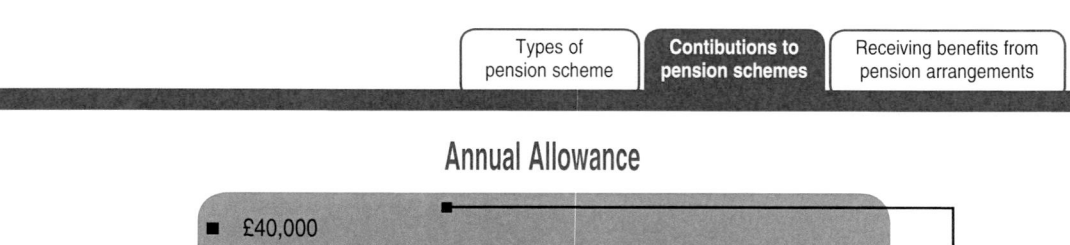

- £40,000
- Tapered annual allowance if adjusted income exceeds £150,000
- Taper allowance by £1 for every £2 of income in excess of £150,000
- Minimum allowance of £10,000 if adjusted income £210,000 or more

Adjusted income = net income if self employed. If employee, add employee occupational scheme contributions and any employer contributions

Tax charge on contributions in excess of the annual allowance

Can c/f unused relief for up to three tax years

Occupational pension

→ Deduct gross employee contributions directly from earnings to find net earnings

Personal pension

→
- Paid net so automatic 20% tax relief
- Higher rate (and additional rate) taxpayers increase basic rate (and higher rate) limits by gross contributions

■ Also deduct gross contributions from net income to find adjusted net income for PA restriction

■ This is the same method of giving tax relief as for gift aid donations

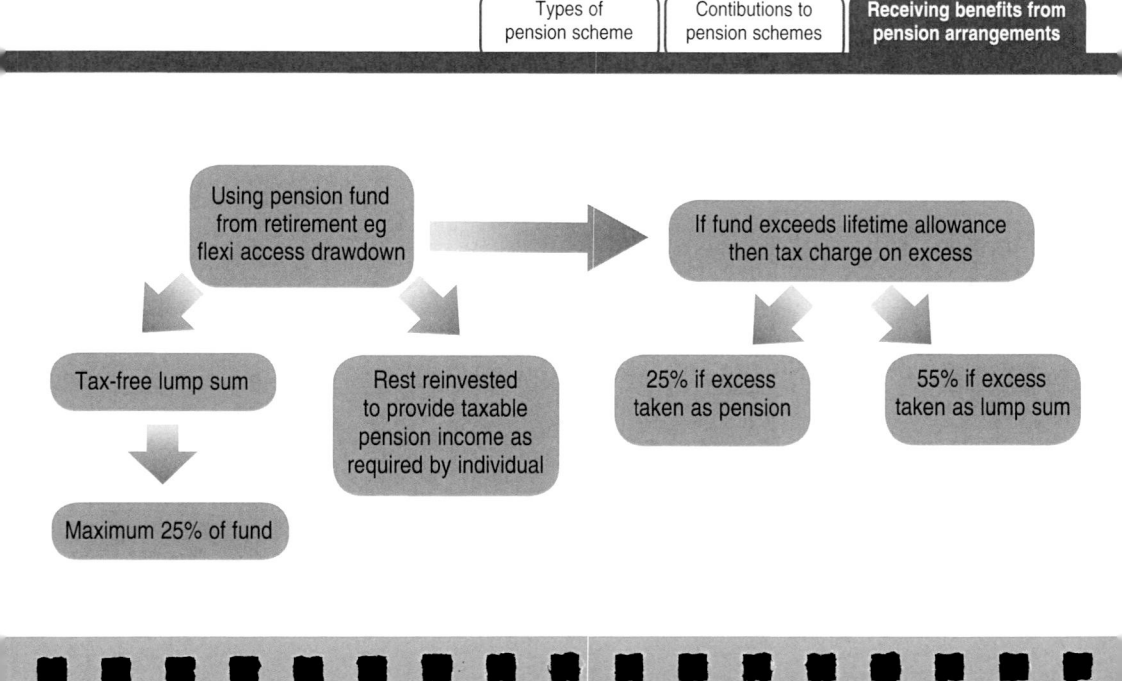

6: Property income

Topic List

Computation

Furnished holiday lettings and rent-a-room relief

Property income is calculated as if the letting were a business run by the taxpayer.

There are special rules for furnished holiday lettings, and for rooms let in the taxpayer's own home.

Property income could be tested in Section A or B and/or in a Section C question, either as a 10 mark question or as part of a 15 mark question.

Property income

Property income covers rent from UK property.

Computation

1. Calculate property business profits for individuals on a cash basis (unless question states accruals basis).

2. Accounts are drawn up as for a sole trader but with a year end of 5 April.

3. Rents and expenses of all properties are pooled to give a single property income figure.

4. If a lease for n years (50 or less) is granted for a premium, the proportion of the premium treated as rent is (premium – (premium × 0.02(n–1))).

Special rules for residential property

1. Finance costs (individuals): restricted to 50%, remaining 50% relieved as tax reducer @ 20%

2. Replacement domestic items relief: for furnished residential lettings

Exception
Keep a separate pool of profits/losses from letting furnished holiday lettings.

Losses

Losses are carried forward against future income from the UK property business.

Furnished holiday lettings

Furnished Holiday Lettings must be:

- On a commercial basis
- Available for letting for 210 days in the tax year
- Actually let for 105 days in the tax year
- Not in **longer term occupation** for more than 155 days during the tax year

- Continuous periods of more than 31 days during which the accommodation is in the same occupation

Furnished holiday lettings are treated as a trade for many income tax and CGT purposes.

- Rollover relief, entrepreneurs' relief and gift relief are available
- Finance costs – no restriction
- Loss relief – but only c/f against FHL profit
- Capital expenditure on furniture allowable when incurred
- Income is earnings for pension purposes

Rent-a-room scheme

The rent-a-room scheme exempts rent of up to £7,500 a year on rooms in the landlord's main residence.

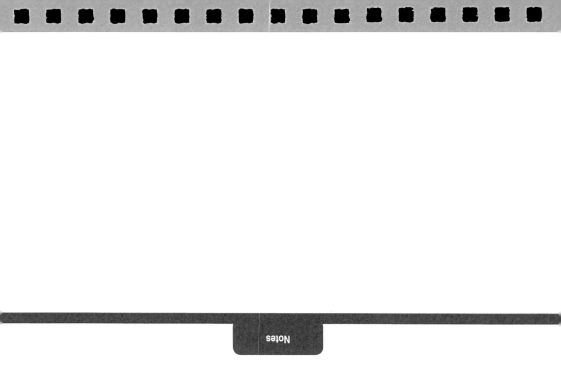

Notes

7: Computing trading income

Topic List

Badges of trade

The adjustment of profits

Cash basis of accounting

The 'badges of trade' can be used to determine whether or not an individual is carrying on a trade. If a trade is being carried on, the profits of the trade are taxable as trading income. Otherwise the profit may be taxable as a capital gain.

In this chapter we will look at the badges of trade and at the adjustments needed in the computation of trading income.

This is a key exam topic. It may form part of a 10 or 15 mark Section C question where you may be required to compute tax adjusted trading profits. Specific adjustments may also be tested in Section A or Section B.

Badges of trade

- The subject matter
- The frequency of transactions
- Similar trading transactions/interests
- The length of ownership
- Organisation as a trade
- Supplementary work and marketing
- A profit motive
- The way in which the asset sold was acquired
- Method of finance
- The taxpayer's intentions

If on applying the badges of trade HMRC conclude that a trade is being carried on, the profits are taxable as trading income.

To arrive at taxable trading profits, the net accounts profit must be adjusted. We look at this in the rest of this chapter.

Certain items of expenditure are not deductible for trading income purposes and so must be added back to the net accounts profit when computing trading profits. Conversely other items are deductible.

Deductible expenditure

- Expenditure incurred **wholly** and **exclusively** for trade purposes
- Gifts to customers not costing more than £50 per donee per year ■ —————— ■ The gift must carry a conspicuous advertisement for the business and not be food, drink, tobacco or vouchers exchangeable for goods.
- Interest on borrowings for trade purposes
- Pre-trading expenditure ■ —————— ■ If incurred in the seven years prior to the start of trade

Non-deductible expenditure

- Fines and penalties ■ ── Employee parking fines incurred whilst on employer's business are, however, allowed

- Depreciation

- Appropriations (eg salary and interest paid to proprietor)

- Capital expenditure ■ ── The cost of initial repairs to make an asset fit to use is disallowable capital expenditure (*Law Shipping*) but the cost of initial repairs to remedy normal wear and tear is allowable (*Odeon Associated Theatres Ltd v Jones*)

- Entertaining ■ ── Staff entertaining is deductible

- Legal fees relating to capital items ■ ── Fees relating to the renewal of a short lease are deductible

- General provisions ■ ── Disallow any general provision for impairment losses. A specific provision is however allowed.

- Any expense not incurred **wholly** and **exclusively** for trade purposes

- Gift aid donations ■ ── These are dealt with in the personal tax computation

- Political donations

- Part of leasing cost of cars with CO_2 emissions over ■ ── Disallow 15% of leasing cost
110g/km

Cash basis of accounting

- Normal basis of accounting is accruals basis
- Cash basis of accounting can be used instead by small unincorporated businesses
- To start cash basis of accounting, receipts must not exceed £150,000
- Election required

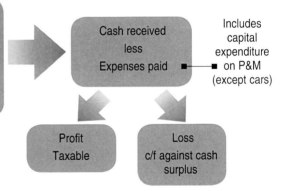

Cash received
less
Expenses paid

Includes capital expenditure on P&M (except cars)

Profit
Taxable

Loss
c/f against cash surplus

Fixed rate expenses ■————————————■ Only examinable in context of cash basis

- Motor cars (business mileage)
- Business premises used as trader's home (eg guesthouse)

Rates given in question where relevant

8: Capital allowances

Topic List

What is plant?

Allowances on plant and machinery

Special assets

Capital allowances are given instead of depreciation, on plant and machinery. They are trading expenses deducted in arriving at taxable trading profits.

Capital allowances are a frequently examined topic.

There are two sources of the rules on what qualifies as plant and is therefore eligible for capital allowances.

Statute

Statutory exclusions

The following items are excluded as plant by statute.

- Buildings and parts of buildings
  - However, utility systems provided to meet the particular requirements of the trade, lifts, alarm systems and several other items can be plant.
- Structures, with some exceptions: dry docks and pipelines
- Land

Statutory inclusions

Computer software qualifies as plant by statute.

Case law

The courts tend to allow items as plant if they perform a function (eg moveable office partitions) in the particular trade, rather than form part of the setting within which the trade is carried on.

Machinery

Machinery also qualifies for allowances where machinery is given its ordinary day every day meaning.

Writing down allowances (WDAs)

- 18% per annum on a reducing balance basis in main pool ■
- WDA given on pool balance after adding current period additions and deducting current period disposals ■
- 18% × months/12 in a period that is not 12 months long
- Reduced WDAs can be claimed
- Expenditure on long life assets, integral features, thermal insulation, solar panels and cars with CO_2 emissions over 110g/km goes in a special rate pool. WDA is 8% per annum on a reducing balance basis
- Small balance (up to £1,000 for 12 month period) on main pool and/or special rate pool can be given WDA equal to balance

> ■ Main pool includes cars with CO_2 emissions 110g/km or less without private use.

> Deduct lower of:
> ■ (i) Disposal proceeds
> (ii) Original cost

Annual Investment Allowance (AIA)

- All businesses are entitled to AIA of £200,000 per 12 month period
- £200,000 maximum allowance is proportionately increased/reduced if period of account is not 12 months
- Allocate AIA to assets eligible for lowest rate of WDA (special rate pool items before main pool items)
- Transfer balance after AIA to pool for same period – WDAs

Expenditure on plant and machinery (although not cars) is entitled to the AIA.

First year allowances (FYAs)

- FYA of 100% available for expenditure on new cars with CO_2 emissions 50g/km or less
- Not pro-rated in short/long period of account

Interaction with VAT

- Expenditure exclusive of input VAT if recoverable
- Expenditure inclusive of input VAT if not recoverable eg car not wholly used for business
- Disposal proceeds exclusive of output VAT

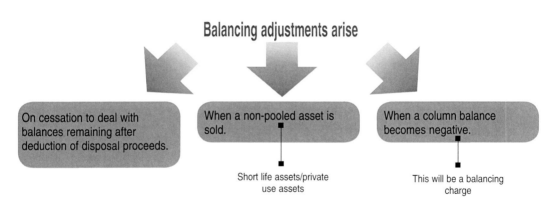

Balancing adjustments arise

On cessation to deal with balances remaining after deduction of disposal proceeds.

When a non-pooled asset is sold.

Short life assets/private use assets

When a column balance becomes negative.

This will be a balancing charge

Short life assets (SLA)

- An **election** can be made to **depool assets.**
- Depooled assets must be disposed of within **eight years** of end of the period of acquisition.
- From a planning point of view depooling is useful if balancing allowances are expected.
- Conversely, in general, assets should not be depooled if they are likely to be sold within eight years for more than their tax written down values.

– Within two years of the end of the accounting period of acquisition (companies)

– 31 Jan, 22 months from end of tax year (unincorporated businesses)

Otherwise the balance of expenditure must be transferred back to pool

Not cars

Private use assets

- Do not pool private use assets
- Show full value of asset/allowances in column
- Can only claim the business proportion of allowances

- Assets used privately by a proprietor (not an employee) so not relevant to companies

9: Assessable trading income

Topic List

Current year basis

Commencement

Cessation

We have seen how to calculate the taxable trading profits for a business. We now see how these profits are allocated to tax years.

This topic may be tested in Section A or B or in a Section C question which could be a 10 mark question or as part of a 15 mark question.

Current year basis

> The basis period for a tax year is normally the period of account ending in the year.

There are special rules which apply in the opening and closing years of a business.

Opening years

Tax year	Basis period
1	Date of commencement to following 5 April.
2	(a) If no accounting date ends in year: 6 April – 5 April (b) If period of account ending in year is less than 12 months: first 12 months (c) Otherwise: 12 months to accounting date ending in Year 2
3	12 months to accounting date ending in year

Overlap profits

> Any profits taxed twice are **overlap profits**. They may be deducted on cessation.

Final year

The basis period for the final year starts at the end of the basis period for the previous year and ends at cessation. Any overlap profits are deducted from the final year's profits.

Example

Brenda has been carrying on a sole trade for many years preparing accounts to 30 April each year. She closes down her business on 30 September 2018. The results of her final two periods of trading are:

	£
y/e 30 April 2018	24,000
p/e 30 September 2018	5,000

Brenda had overlap profits on commencement of £10,000.

The final year is 2018/19 and the basis period for this year runs from 1 May 2017 to 30 September 2018. She can deduct the overlap profits. Her taxable trading income for 2018/19 is therefore £(24,000 + 5,000 – 10,000) = £19,000.

10: Trading losses

Topic List

Carry forward of trading losses

Set against general income

Opening and closing years

This is another key exam topic. It is likely to be tested in Section C but specific aspects, such as the restriction on losses set against general income, may be tested in Sections A or B.

There is no general rule that sole traders can get relief for their losses. The conditions of a specific relief must be complied with. We look at these reliefs in this chapter.

Carry forward trading loss relief

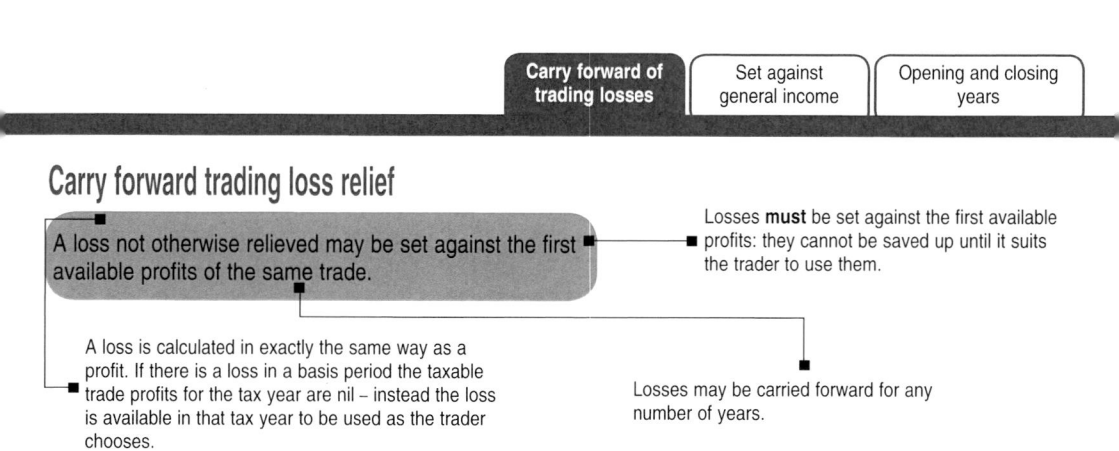

A loss not otherwise relieved may be set against the first available profits of the same trade.

Losses **must** be set against the first available profits: they cannot be saved up until it suits the trader to use them.

A loss is calculated in exactly the same way as a profit. If there is a loss in a basis period the taxable trade profits for the tax year are nil – instead the loss is available in that tax year to be used as the trader chooses.

Losses may be carried forward for any number of years.

| Carry forward of trading losses | **Set against general income** | Opening and closing years |

Example

Sue starts trading on 1.10.18. Her losses are:
| y/e 30.9.19 | £(50,000) |
| y/e 30.9.20 | £(20,000) |

Losses for the tax years are:
2018/19	£(25,000)
2019/20	£(50,000 – 25,000) = £(25,000)
2020/21	£(20,000)

Losses in two overlapping basis periods are given to the earlier tax year only.

Relief against general income

Relief is against the **income of the tax year of the loss and/or the preceding tax year**.

Partial claims are not allowed: the whole loss must be set off, if there is income (or, if chosen, gains) to absorb it in the chosen tax year.

Relief against non-trading income restricted to greater of 25% of adjusted total income and £50,000

Can extend the claim to net gains of the same year, less brought forward capital losses.

Exam focus

Before recommending relief against general income, consider whether it would lead to the waste of the personal allowance. This is often a significant tax planning point.

Opening years

A loss incurred in the first **four** years of trade can be set against general income of the **three** preceding years under early years trade losses relief.

Relief is given in the earliest year first (FIFO)

Closing years

A loss incurred in the last **12 months** of trade can be set against trading profits in the year of cessation and in the **three** preceding years under terminal loss relief.

Relief is given in the latest year first (LIFO)

Computation of loss

Take the loss of the last tax year (6 April to date of cessation) plus the proportion of the loss in the preceding tax year corresponding to the period from 12 months before cessation to 5 April.

Add overlap profits to the loss in the last year.

11: Partnerships and limited liability partnerships

Topic List

Sharing profits between partners

Losses

Partnerships are another key exam topic. You should be prepared to answer a Section C question on this topic, although it may also be tested in Section A or in Section B. The technique is to allocate the profits between the partners and then look at each partner independently.

Compute trading results for a partnership as a whole in the same way as you would compute the profits for a sole trader

then

Divide results for each period of account between partners

First allocate salaries and interest on capital to the partners, then share the balance of profits among the partners according to the profit-sharing ratio for the period of account

Each partner is taxed as if they were running their own business, and making profits and losses equal to their share of the firm's results for each period of account

Remember to pro-rate the annual salary/interest if the period is not 12 months long.

When a partner joins, the first period of account for their own business runs from the date of joining to the firm's next accounting date. The normal basis period rules for opening years apply to them.

When a partner leaves, the last period of account for their own business runs from the firm's most recent accounting date to the day they leave. The normal cessation rules apply to them.

Losses

Partners are entitled to the same loss reliefs as sole traders:

1 Divide the loss for each period of account between the partners

2 Next calculate the loss for each tax year

3 Consider all available loss reliefs for each individual partner

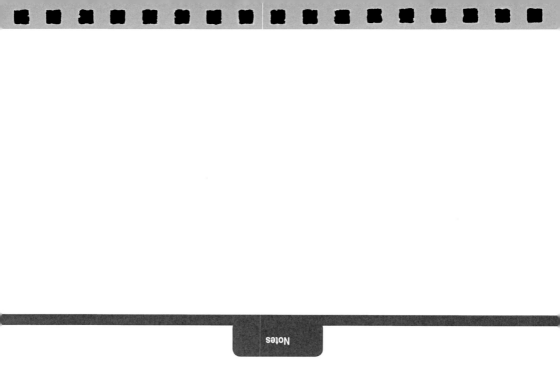

Notes

12: National insurance contributions

Topic List

NICs for employees

NICs for the self-employed

Although often overlooked, national insurance contributions represent a significant cost to taxpayers.

National insurance contributions could be tested in Section A and also as part of a Section B or Section C question.

CLASS 1

Employee

Employees pay contributions of 12% of earnings between the employee's threshold and the upper earnings limit. 2% on earnings above the upper limit.

- Not reduced by expenses or pension contributions.

Employer

Employers pay contributions of 13.8% on all earnings above the employee's threshold.

- Employment allowance reduction up to £3,000 per employer for tax year (not if sole employee/director).

CLASS 1A

Employers pay Class 1A contributions at 13.8% on most taxable benefits provided for their employees. Class 1A is payable on 22 July if electronic payment (19 July if by cheque) following the end of the tax year.

Exam focus

The earnings thresholds and the upper earnings limit will be given to you in the exam.

The self-employed pay Class 2 and Class 4 NICs.

Class 2

Class 2 are paid at a flat weekly rate. Paid under self assessment. Due by 31 January after end of tax year.

Class 4

Class 4 NICs are 9% of any profits falling between a lower and an upper limit and 2% above upper limit. Class 4 NICs are collected at the same time as the associated income tax liability.

Exam focus

In questions which ask whether someone should trade as a sole trader or through a company (as a director) the cost of NICs often tips the balance in favour of being a sole trader.

■ Profits are the taxable profits, as reduced by trading losses. Personal pension contributions do not reduce profits.

■ These limits will be given to you on the exam paper.

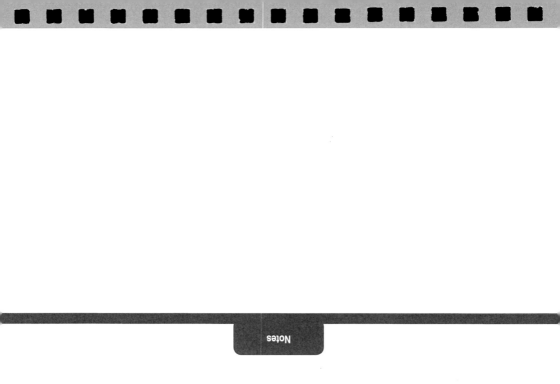

Notes

13: Computing chargeable gains

Topic List

Chargeable persons, disposals and assets

Basic computation

Losses

The charge to CGT for individuals

Spouses and civil partners

Part disposals

Damage, loss or destruction

It is important that you can calculate chargeable gains realised by individuals and calculate their capital gains tax liability having dealt with losses and the offset of the annual exempt amount.

You may find that the basic topics in this chapter are tested in Section A and you should also be prepared to answer a Section B or Section C question containing a number of disposals of chargeable assets.

Chargeable persons, disposals and assets

Three elements are needed for a chargeable gain to arise:

1 A **chargeable disposal**: this includes sales, gifts and the destruction of assets. Transfer of assets on death is not chargeable.

2 A **chargeable person**: individuals are chargeable persons.

CGT applies primarily to persons resident in the UK

3 A **chargeable asset**: most assets are chargeable, but some assets are exempt.

Cars
Some chattels (eg racehorses)
Gilts
QCBs

Computation

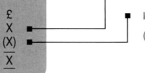

Compute a gain as follows:

	£
Proceeds	X
Less cost	(X)
Gain	X

■ **Actual proceeds** or **market value** in the case of gifts and disposals which are not bargains at arms length.

■ Include:

(1) **Original cost** of the asset or **market value** if that was used as proceeds for the person who sold the asset to this individual.

(2) **Enhancement expenditure** which was reflected in the state and nature of the asset at the time of disposal or was on preserving the owner's legal right to the asset.

(3) **Incidental costs** of **acquisition** and **disposal.**

Order of set off

1. Residential property gains
2. Other gains without entrepreneurs' relief
3. Entrepreneurs' relief gains

Deduct allowable capital losses from gains in the tax year in which they arise (before deducting the annual exempt amount).

Allowable losses brought forward are only set off to reduce current year gains less current year allowable losses to the annual exempt amount.

Any loss which cannot be set off is carried forward to set against future gains.

Example

Zoë made gains of £14,700 in 2018/19. She had brought forward capital losses of £8,000.

Brought forward capital losses of £3,000 will be set off in 2018/19 to preserve annual exempt amount of £11,700. The remaining losses will be carried forward to 2019/20.

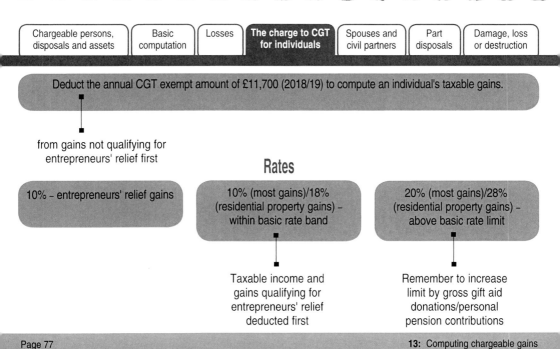

Deduct the annual CGT exempt amount of £11,700 (2018/19) to compute an individual's taxable gains.

from gains not qualifying for entrepreneurs' relief first

Rates

10% – entrepreneurs' relief gains

10% (most gains)/18% (residential property gains) – within basic rate band

20% (most gains)/28% (residential property gains) – above basic rate limit

Taxable income and gains qualifying for entrepreneurs' relief deducted first

Remember to increase limit by gross gift aid donations/personal pension contributions

No gain/no loss disposals

Disposals between spouses and civil partners do not give rise to gains or losses.

When the second spouse/civil partner sells the asset, assume that they bought the asset for its original cost.

Part disposals

On a part disposal, you are only allowed to take part of the cost of the asset into account.

- Costs attributable solely to the part disposed of are taken into account in full
- For other costs, take into account A/(A+B) of the cost:
  - A is the proceeds of the part sold
  - B is the market value of the part retained

Example

X owns land which originally cost £30,000. It sold a quarter interest in the land for £18,000. The incidental costs of disposal were £1,000. The market value of the three-quarter share remaining is estimated to be £36,000. What is the chargeable gain?

	£
Proceeds	18,000
Less incidental costs of disposal	(1,000)
	17,000
Less $\dfrac{18,000}{18,000 + 36,000} \times 30,000$	(10,000)
	7,000

Damage

If an asset is damaged and compensation is received, then this will normally be treated as a part disposal.

↓

If all the proceeds are used to restore the asset the taxpayer can elect to disregard the part disposal and deduct the proceeds from the cost of the asset.

Loss or destruction

If an asset is destroyed any compensation will normally be brought into an ordinary CGT disposal computation as proceeds.

↓

If all the proceeds are applied for the replacement of the asset within 12 months, any gain can be deducted from the cost of the replacement asset.

↓

If only part of the proceeds are applied, the gain is restricted to the part not applied, and the remainder of the gain is deducted from the cost of the replacement asset.

14: Chattels and the principal private residence exemption

Topic List

Chattels

Wasting assets

Private residences

In this chapter we look at the rules which apply for calculating the gains on certain special types of asset.

The chattel rules may well be tested in Section A. The rules on private residences could form part of a Section B or Section C question.

Chattels

A chattel is an item of **tangible moveable property** (eg a painting).

Gains on chattels sold for gross proceeds of £6,000 or less are exempt.

The maximum gain on chattels sold for more than £6,000 is 5/3 (gross proceeds – £6,000).

Losses on chattels sold for under £6,000 are restricted by assuming the gross proceeds to be £6,000.

Wasting chattels

Wasting chattels are exempt from CGT unless capital allowances could have been claimed on them.

- Chattels with a remaining estimated useful life of 50 years or less.

Wasting asset

A wasting asset is one with an estimated remaining useful life of 50 years or less and whose original value will fall over time.

Wasting assets have their cost written down over time on a straight line basis.

Exception

Assets eligible for capital allowances and used in a trade do not have their cost written down.

Example

Jo bought a copyright with a remaining life of 40 years for £10,000. He sold the copyright 15 years later for £30,000. Calculate the gain arising.

	£
Proceeds	30,000
Less cost (£10,000 × 25/40)	(6,250)
Gain	23,750

- Number of years remaining
- Number of years on acquisition

Principal private residence relief

A gain on the disposal of a PPR is wholly exempt where the owner has occupied the whole residence throughout their period of ownership.

Where occupation has been for only part of a period, the proportion of the gain exempted is

$$\text{Gain} \times \frac{\text{Period of occupation}}{\text{Total period of ownership}}$$

Periods of deemed occupation

- Absences totalling up to three years for any reason
- Absences while employed abroad
- Absences totalling up to four years while working elsewhere

These periods must normally be preceded and followed by a period of actual occupation

- The last 18 months of ownership of a residence is always treated as a period of deemed occupation.

Provided that there is no other main residence at the time

Exam focus

Draw up a table of periods present or absent, exempt months and chargeable months. Check that the total of exempt and chargeable months is correct, to avoid making mistakes.

Business use

When part of residence is used exclusively for business purposes, that part of gain is taxable. Last 18 months exemption does not apply.

Letting exemption

A gain arising whilst a PPR is let is exempt up to the lower of:

1. £40,000

2. The amount of the PPR exemption

3. The gain in the let period

Permitted area

The private residence exemption covers a house plus up to half a hectare of grounds. A larger area may be allowed for substantial houses.

14: Chattels and the principal private residence exemption

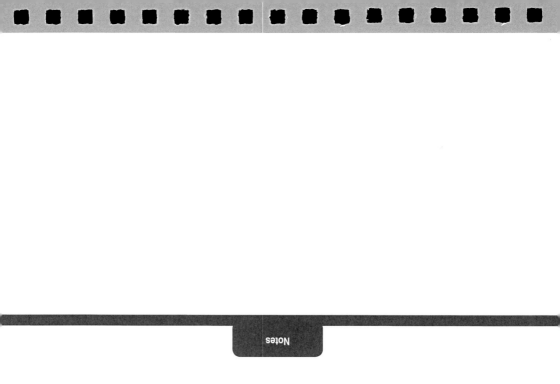

Notes

15: Business reliefs

Topic List

Entrepreneurs' relief

Rollover relief

Gift relief

In a Section C exam question you should look out for the availability of various reliefs. However, do take care to ensure that you do not claim relief when you are not allowed to.

Entrepreneurs' relief

Claim by 12 months from 31 January following tax year of disposal

Available for material disposal of business assets

Business owned for one year prior to disposal or business has ceased within past three years and business owned at least one year prior to cessation

Tax net gains at 10%
Lifetime limit of £10m gains

Business assets

- Sole trader business/partnership
- Shares in 'personal' trading company owned by employee/officer

'Personal' trading company requires shareholding/voting rights of at least 5%

Must be the disposal of the whole or part of the business, not just individual assets if business continues

Investors' relief

- Similar to entrepreneurs' relief
- 10% rate of tax regardless of income
- Investor acquires newly issued shares in unlisted trading companies by subscription (no minimum shareholding) on or after 17 March 2016
- Investor must own shares for at least three years from the later of 6 April 2016 and the date of the issue of the shares until the date of disposal
- Investor must not usually be director or employee of company
- Lifetime limit £10,000,000 (separate from entrepreneurs' relief limit)

Computational aspects not examinable until tax year 2019/20

Taxpayers can claim to defer gains arising on the disposal of business assets that are being replaced if both the old and the new assets are on the list of eligible assets.

The new asset must be bought in the period starting 12 months before and ending 36 months after the disposal.

Exam focus

If a question mentions the sale of some business assets and the purchase of others, look out for rollover relief but do not just assume that it is available: the assets might be of the wrong type, eg moveable plant and machinery.

Eligible assets

- Land and buildings (including parts of buildings) occupied as well as used only for the purposes of the trade.
- Fixed (that is, immovable) plant and machinery.
- Goodwill

A depreciating asset is one with an expected life of 60 years or less (eg fixed plant and machinery).

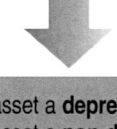

Is the new asset a **depreciating** asset?
Is the new asset a **non-depreciating** asset?

For a non-depreciating asset the gain is deducted from the base cost of the new asset.

For a depreciating asset the gain is deferred until it crystallises at a later date.

If a part of the proceeds of the old asset are not reinvested, the gain is chargeable up to the amount not reinvested.

The gain crystallises on the earliest of:

1. The disposal of the replacement asset

2. Ten years after the acquisition of the replacement asset

3. The date the replacement asset ceases to be used in the trade

Relief is proportionately restricted when an asset has not been used for trade purposes throughout its life.

If a non-depreciating qualifying asset is bought before the gain crystallises, the deferred gain may be rolled into the base cost of that asset.

15: Business reliefs

Gift relief

Gift relief may be claimed to defer gains arising on business assets.

↓

The gain is deducted from the recipient's base cost.

↓

Any actual proceeds in excess of cost reduce the gain for which relief can be claimed.

→

Qualifying assets

- Assets used in a trade
- Shares and securities in trading company which is either unlisted or the donor's personal company

- If the company holds non-business assets, gain eligible for gift relief restricted to CBA/CA × gain

16: Shares and securities

Topic List

Matching

The computation

Alterations of share capital

The matching rules for shares and securities are vitally important, in particular in a Section C question. If you do not know the matching rules you will not be able to compute a gain on the disposal of shares.

The matching rules for shares held by an individual are different to the matching rules for shares held by a company. Take care not to confuse the two.

Matching rules for individuals

Disposals by individual shareholders are matched with acquisitions in the following order:

- Same day acquisitions
- Acquisitions within the following 30 days
- Any shares in the share pool

Exam focus

Learn the 'matching rules' because a crucial first step to getting a shares question right is to correctly match the shares sold to the original shares purchased.

The computation

The computation is proceeds less cost.

For disposal of quoted shares at MV (eg gift) proceeds are calculated as the lower of the two prices shown in the Stock Exchange Daily Official List plus one-half of the difference between those two prices.

The share pool

The share pool is kept in two columns:

1 The **number** of shares

2 The **cost**

On a disposal the cost is calculated on a pro-rata basis.

Bonus issues

- Bonus issue shares are acquired at no cost.
- Add the number of shares to the share pool.

Rights issues

- Rights issue shares are acquired for payment.
- Add the numbers of shares to the share pool and add the cost of the rights shares.

Reorganisations and takeovers

- Apportion the cost of the old shares to the new assets received in proportion to their values.
- Where the new assets include cash, compute a chargeable gain using the cash received and the part of the cost of the old shares apportioned to that cash.
- Takeover must be for bona fide commercial reasons and not for tax avoidance for this treatment to apply.

17: Self-assessment and payment of tax by individuals

Topic List

Returns

Records and appeals

Payment of tax

Penalties

This is a key exam topic. It may be examined in a Section A or Section B question or in a Section C question either as part of a 15 mark question focused on income tax or in a 10 mark question.

Filing date

The latest filing date for filing a 2018/19 tax return is:

(1) 31 October 2019 (paper)
(2) 31 January 2020 (electronic)

Exception: if notice after 31 July 2019, latest filing date is end of three months after notice

Exception: if notice after 31 October 2019, latest filing date is end of three months after notice

Compliance checks

HMRC randomly select returns to check. They also select returns where there is an identified tax risk.

HMRC may make a compliance check enquiry into a return provided they give notice by a year after:

(1) The actual filing date (if on or before due filing date)
(2) The 31 January, 30 April, 31 July or 31 October next following the actual filing date of the return (if filed late).

Records

Records must, in general, be kept until the later of:

(1) Five years after the 31 January following the tax year concerned (where the taxpayer is in business); or

(2) One year after the 31 January following the tax year, otherwise.

Appeals

- A taxpayer may appeal against:
    - Any assessment, except a self-assessment
    - An amendment to a self-assessment or a disallowance of a claim or election, following a compliance check or discovery
    - Penalties
- The appeal may be settled by internal review. If not, the hearing is before Tax Tribunal.

Powers

- HMRC can investigate dishonest conduct by tax agent – penalty up to £50,000.
- HMRC may make assessments to recover tax due and determinations which effectively force the filing of a return.

Payment of tax

Payments on account (POA) of income tax and Class 4 NICs must be made on 31 January in tax year and on the following 31 July.

The final payment of income tax and Class 4 NICs must be paid on 31 January following the tax year.

All CGT and Class 2 NIC is due on 31 January following the tax year.

- Each POA is 50% of the prior tax year's income tax and Class 4 NIC liability less tax suffered at source (de minimis limits £1,000, 80%)

Interest

Interest runs on:

(1) POAs from the normal due dates (31 Jan and 31 July).

(2) Any final payment and CGT from the later of:

    (i) 31 January following tax year

    (ii) Three months after the notice to file a tax return was issued

Penalties for errors

- Common penalty regime for IT, NICs, CT and VAT

- Imposed for inaccurate return leading to understatement of tax, false or increased loss, false or increased repayment of tax

- Error may be careless, deliberate but not concealed, or deliberate and concealed

Maximum penalty based on Potential Lost Revenues (PLR):

- 100% if deliberate and concealed
- 70% if deliberate but not concealed
- 30% if careless

Penalties can be reduced by disclosure (eg 0% for careless error with unprompted disclosure)

Penalties for late notification

- Common penalty regime for IT, NICs, PAYE, CGT, CT and VAT
- Failure may be careless, deliberate but not concealed, or deliberate and concealed
- Maximum penalty based on PLR as for penalties for error
- Reduced penalties for disclosure: eg 0% if careless failure with unprompted disclosure within 12 months

Penalty for failure to keep records

£3,000 per tax year/accounting period

Penalties for late filing

The maximum penalties for delivering a return after the filing due date are:

(1)	Return up to three months late	£100
(2)	Return over three months late	As (1) plus £10 daily penalty (max 90 days)
(3)	Return over six months late	As (1) and (2) plus greater of 5% of tax and £300
(4)	Return over 12 months late	As (1), (2), (3) plus greater of % of tax (conduct related) and £300

Penalties for late payment

(1) Penalty date is 30 days after due date

(2) Penalty of 5% of unpaid tax at penalty date if payment not more than five months after penalty date

(3) Penalty of 5% of unpaid tax at five months after penalty date if payment between five months and 11 months of penalty date

(4) Penalty of 5% of unpaid tax at 11 months after penalty date if payment more than 11 months after penalty date

(5) Does not apply to payments on account

18: Inheritance tax: scope and transfers of value

Topic List

Scope/basic principles

Exemptions

CLTs and PETs

Death estate

Transfer of nil rate bands

Payment of IHT

Inheritance tax is a tax on transfer of wealth (gifts). It applies to certain gifts made during lifetime and on death. Inheritance tax may be examined in Sections A or B and/or in a 10 mark Section C question.

Scope of inheritance tax

Transfer of value

By individuals

Lifetime or death

For Taxation (UK) a gift

Transfer of value

A gratuitous disposition which results in an individual being worse off.

Diminution in value

Usually = gift but watch out for unquoted shares (before/after)

The value of the transfer is always the loss to the donor.

Seven-year accumulation principle

Need to look back seven years from chargeable transfer to see if any chargeable transfers use up available nil rate band.

2018/19 £325,000

Chargeable transfer

Any transfer which is not an exempt transfer.

Chargeable lifetime transfer (CLT) – immediate charge to tax. Gift to trust.

Potentially exempt transfer (PET) only chargeable if donor does not survive seven years – treat as exempt until death. Gift to individual (except spouse/civil partner).

Chargeable transfer on death.

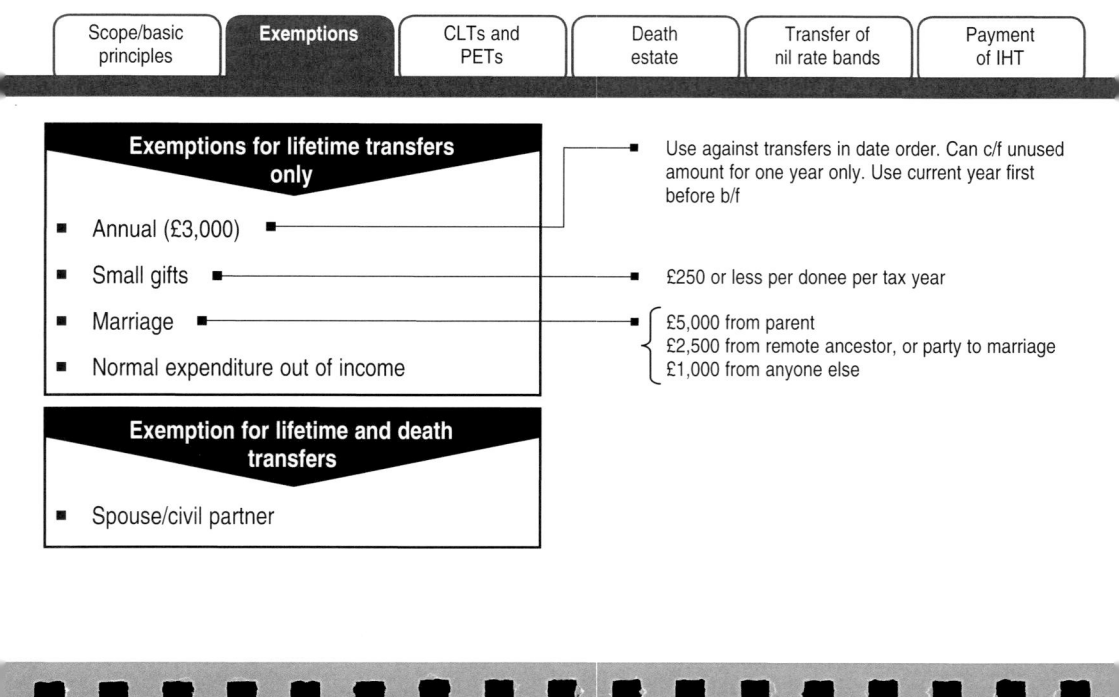

Exemptions for lifetime transfers only

- Annual (£3,000)
- Small gifts
- Marriage
- Normal expenditure out of income

- Use against transfers in date order. Can c/f unused amount for one year only. Use current year first before b/f

- £250 or less per donee per tax year

- £5,000 from parent
  £2,500 from remote ancestor, or party to marriage
  £1,000 from anyone else

Exemption for lifetime and death transfers

- Spouse/civil partner

| Scope/basic principles | Exemptions | **CLTs and PETs** | Death estate | Transfer of nil rate bands | Payment of IHT |

Chargeable lifetime transfers (CLTs)

IHT charged at date of gift at 20% if exceeds nil rate band at date of gift.

Gross up (20/80) if donor pays lifetime tax as they have lost both the gift and the IHT paid.

Additional tax on death

The IHT on death on a CLT made in seven years before death is calculated as follows:

(1) Take into account all chargeable transfers in seven yrs before this transfer (including PETs which have become chargeable)

(2) Calculate the tax at 40% on excess of the gross CLT over nil rate band at death

(3) Deduct taper relief if death between three–seven yrs after transfer

(4) Deduct lifetime tax – but no repayment if exceeds tapered death tax

Exam focus

When you have grossed up a transfer, you can check your figures by computing the 20% tax on the gross transfer.

Potentially Exempt Transfers (PETs)

Treat as exempt during lifetime of donor ■━━━━■ If donor does survive seven years from transfer, PET is exempt transfer.

Tax on death

IHT on a PET made in seven years before death is calculated as follows:

(1) Take into account all chargeable transfers in seven years before this transfer (including other PETs which have become chargeable)

(2) Calculate tax @ 40% on excess over nil rate band at death

(3) Deduct taper relief if death between three and seven years after transfer

Death estate

- All property owned immediately before death
- Less debts, funeral expenses ■━━━━━━━━━ ■ Including cost of tombstone

■ Incurred for consideration or imposed by law (eg tax to date of death)

Debt secured on property, eg mortgage

- Deducted primarily from secured property, eg house

- Endowment mortgages not deducted as repaid on death by insurance

- Repayment/interest only mortgages are deductible (may be separate life cover)

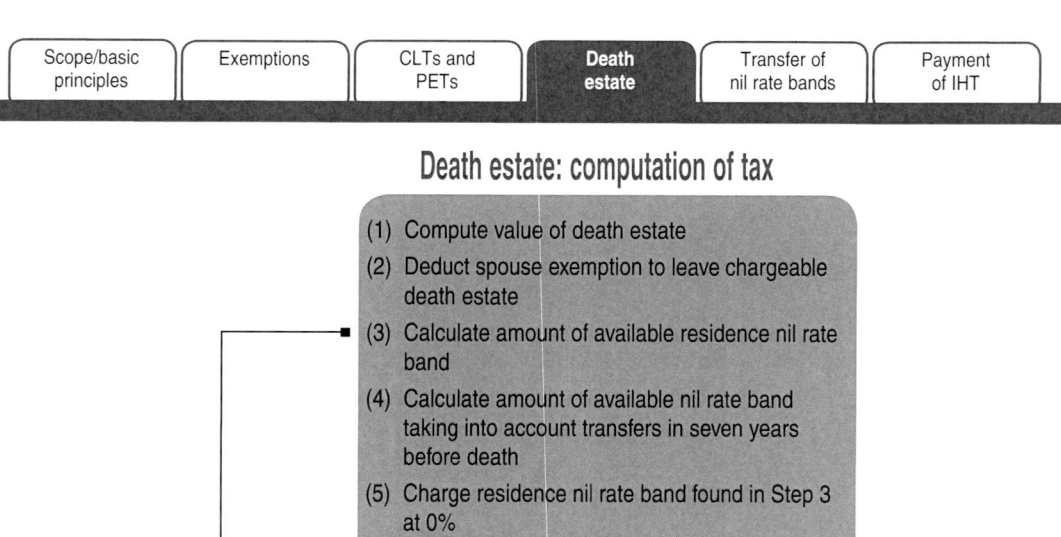

Death estate: computation of tax

(1) Compute value of death estate

(2) Deduct spouse exemption to leave chargeable death estate

(3) Calculate amount of available residence nil rate band

(4) Calculate amount of available nil rate band taking into account transfers in seven years before death

(5) Charge residence nil rate band found in Step 3 at 0%

(6) Charge nil rate band found in Step 4 at 0%

(7) Charge remainder of death estate at 40%

Lower of maximum residence nil rate band and net value of main residence

Transfer of unused nil rate bands

- Individual (A) dies
- A had spouse/civil partner (B) who died before A
- B had unused nil rate bands on death

Deemed residence nil rate band £125,000 (2018/19) if B died before 6.4.17

Effect

- Maximum nil rate bands of A increased by unused nil rate bands of B
- Nil rate band affects additional tax on CLTs, tax on PETs and death estate, residence nil rate band affects death estate only
- Scale up if nil rate bands increased between B's death and A's death

Claim

Within two years of end of month of A's death by A's PRs.

Payment of IHT

Event	Liability to pay tax	Due date
CLT – lifetime tax	Donor unless trustees agree to pay	Later of (1) 30 April just after end of tax year (2) Six months after end of month of transfer
CLT – death tax	Trustees	Six months from end of month of donor's death
PET	Donee	Six months from end of month of donor's death
Death estate	PRs	Earlier of (1) Delivery of account (2) Six months from end of month of donor's death

19: Computing taxable total profits and the corporation tax liability

Topic List

Accounting periods

Residence

Taxable total profits

Trading profits and property business income

Loan relationships

Long period of account

Computing corporation tax

In this chapter we will cover the structure of the computation of taxable total profits and the calculation of the corporation tax liability. This is an essential part of your examination as one 15 mark Section C question will focus on corporation tax. Specific aspects of corporation tax may also be examined in Sections A or B.

Period of account

A period of account is the period for which accounts are prepared.

Accounting period

An accounting period is the period for which corporation tax is charged.

An accounting period can never exceed 12 months. If a company prepares accounts for a period exceeding 12 months, the period of account must be split into 2 accounting periods.

- It starts when the company starts to trade, or immediately after the end of the previous accounting period.

- It ends 12 months after it starts or, if earlier, when the period of account ends.

The first 12 months form the first accounting period

The remaining months form the second accounting period

Residence

A company is resident in the UK if it is incorporated in the UK or if its central management and control are in the UK.

A UK resident company is subject to UK corporation tax on its worldwide profits.

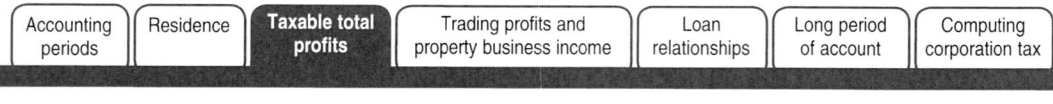

| Accounting periods | Residence | **Taxable total profits** | Trading profits and property business income | Loan relationships | Long period of account | Computing corporation tax |

Taxable total profits

A company's taxable total profits are arrived at by aggregating its various sources of income and chargeable gains (total profits) and then deducting qualifying charitable donations and certain losses.

Profits of trades ■

Interest from non-trading loan relationships ■
(eg bank/building society interest)

Any other profits ■

Income from land and buildings in the UK ■

Proforma for calculating taxable total profits

	£
Trading profits	X
Interest income	X
Miscellaneous income	X
Property business income	X
Chargeable gains	X
Total profits	X
Less losses	(X)
Less qualifying charitable donations	(X)
Taxable total profits	X

Dividends from other companies are not included in taxable total profits.

Trading profits

The computation of trading profits follows income tax principles.

Remember there is no disallowance of expenditure or restriction of capital allowances for private use.

Property business income

The computation of property business income follows income tax principles (accruals basis).

- **Exception:** Interest on a loan taken out to buy property is dealt with under the loan relationship rules, not as part of the property business. No restriction on finance costs.

Proforma

	£	£
Net profit per accounts		X
Add expenditure not allowed for tax purposes		X
		X
Deduct		
Income not taxable as trading income	X	
Expenditure not charged in the accounts but allowable for tax	X	
Capital allowances	X	
		(X)
Taxable trading profits		X

Loan relationships

A company that borrows or invests money has a loan relationship.

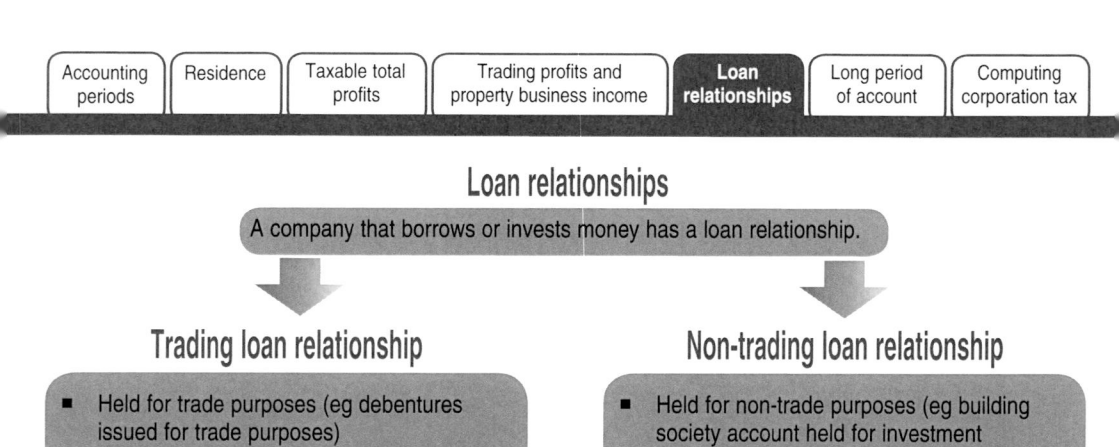

Trading loan relationship

- Held for trade purposes (eg debentures issued for trade purposes)
- Costs (eg interest) accruing are deductible trading income expenses
- Income accruing (eg interest income) is taxable as trading income

Non-trading loan relationship

- Held for non-trade purposes (eg building society account held for investment purposes)
- Tax income accruing as interest income
- Deduct expenses accruing from the pool of interest income

    Net deficits are not examinable

Long period of account (> 12 months)

The first 12 months form the first accounting period

The remaining months form the second accounting period

Example

If A Ltd prepares accounts for the fifteen months to 31.12.18, there will be one 12 month accounting period to 30.9.18 and a second three month accounting period to 31.12.18.

Division of profits

Divide profits between the accounting periods as follows:

- Trading income: time apportion the amount before capital allowances
- Compute capital allowances separately for each period
- Property business income: time apportion
- Interest income: allocate to period in which it accrues
- Miscellaneous income: time apportion
- Gains: allocate to the period in which they are realised
- Qualifying charitable donations: allocate to the period in which they are paid

- Rate of corporation tax set for financial years.
- Rate of corporation tax for financial year 2018 is 19%.
- Rate applied to taxable total profits to compute corporation tax liability.
- If accounting period spans 1 April and different rates of corporation tax in financial years either side, time apportion taxable total profits to each financial year and apply rates separately.

A financial year runs from 1 April in one year to 31 March in the next. Financial Year 2018 (FY 2018) runs from 1 April 2018 to 31 March 2019.

20: Chargeable gains for companies

Topic List

Calculation of chargeable gains

Disposal of shares

Rollover relief

This chapter deals with calculating chargeable gains for companies.

A key area is the rules for the disposal of shares and securities.

Computation

Compute a gain as follows:

	£
Proceeds	X
Less allowable cost	(X)
Less indexation allowance	(X)
Chargeable gain	X

(1) Cannot create or increase a loss
(2) Will be given indexation factor in question

RPI for earlier of month of disposal/December 2017 –
RPI for month of acquisition

RPI for month of acquisition

1 Include in total profits, and so charged to corporation tax

2 No annual exempt amount

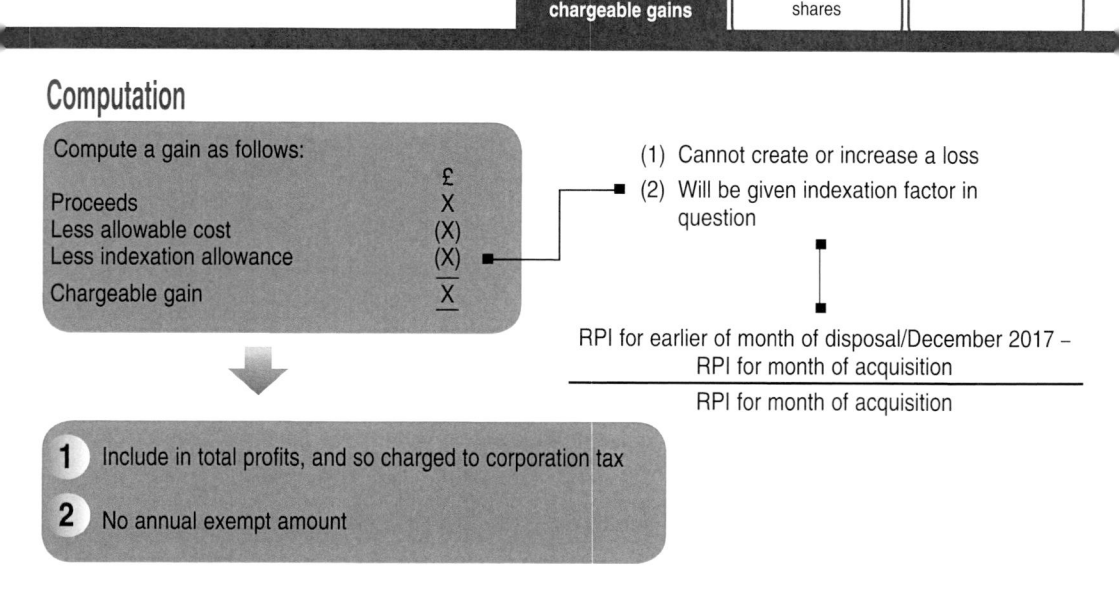

Shares and securities

For company shareholders disposals of shares and securities are matched with acquisitions in the following order:

(i) Shares acquired on the same day

(ii) Shares acquired in the previous nine days, taking earlier acquisitions first

(iii) Shares from the FA 1985 pool

The FA 1985 pool is kept in three columns:

1 The **number** of shares

2 The **cost**

3 The **indexed cost**

Operative event

Operative events are acquisitions and disposals (apart from bonus issues)

At each operative event:

(1) Increase the indexed cost column by the indexed rise since the date of the last operative event; then

(2) Add the cost of any shares acquired to both the cost/indexed cost columns; or

The indexation allowance is the indexed cost taken out of the indexed cost column minus the cost taken out of the cost column.

(3) Deduct a pro-rata slice from the cost/indexed cost columns in respect of any shares disposed of.

Reorganisations and takeovers

- Apportion the cost and indexed cost of the old shares to the new assets received in proportion to their values.

- Where the new assets include cash, compute a chargeable gain using the cash received and the parts of the cost and indexed cost of the old shares apportioned to that cash.

- If just a takeover qualifying for the 'paper for paper' treatment, the cost and indexed cost of the original holding is passed onto the new holding which now takes its place.

Companies can claim to defer gains arising on the disposal of business assets that are being replaced if:

1 The old and the new assets are used in the trade of the company.

2 The old and the new assets are on the list of qualifying assets.

3 The new asset is bought in the period starting 12 months before and ending 36 months after the disposal.

Eligible assets

- Land and buildings (including parts of buildings) occupied as well as used only for the purposes of the trade.
- Fixed (that is, immovable) plant and machinery.

A depreciating asset is one with an expected life of 60 years or less (eg fixed plant and machinery).

Is the new asset a **depreciating** asset?
Is the new asset a **non-depreciating** asset?

For a non-depreciating asset the gain is deducted from the base cost of the new asset.

For a depreciating asset the gain is deferred until it crystallises at a later date.

If a part of the proceeds of the old asset are not reinvested, the gain is chargeable up to the amount not reinvested.

The gain crystallises on the earliest of:

1. The disposal of the replacement asset

2. Ten years after the acquisition of the replacement asset

3. The date the replacement asset ceases to be used in the trade

Relief is proportionately restricted when an asset has not been used for trade purposes throughout its life.

If a non-depreciating qualifying asset is bought before the gain crystallises, the deferred gain may be rolled into the base cost of that asset.

20: Chargeable gains for companies

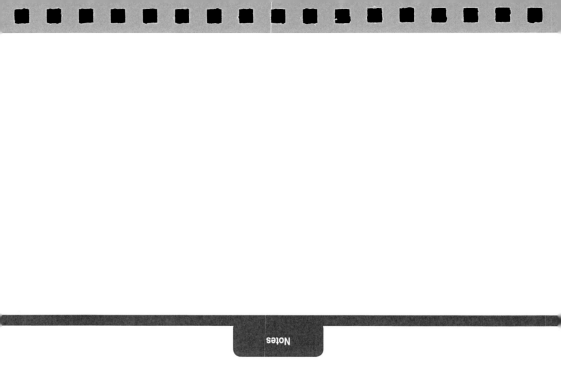

Notes

21: Losses

Topic List

Trading losses

Non-trading losses

In this chapter we will see how a single company may obtain tax relief for its trading and non-trading losses. Losses are a key topic area for exam purposes. The best way of learning how to deal with losses is to practise questions involving losses in the BPP Learning Media Practice & Revision Kit.

Trading losses

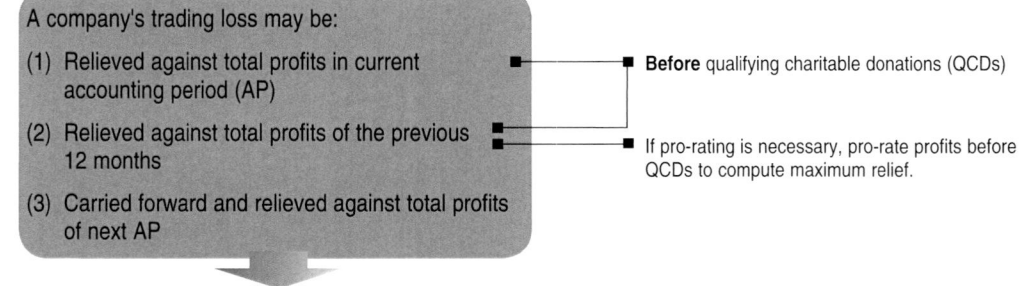

A company's trading loss may be:

(1) Relieved against total profits in current accounting period (AP)

(2) Relieved against total profits of the previous 12 months

(3) Carried forward and relieved against total profits of next AP

Before qualifying charitable donations (QCDs)

If pro-rating is necessary, pro-rate profits before QCDs to compute maximum relief.

Reliefs (1) and (2) need to be claimed. A company can choose to claim relief (1) only (ie relief (1) but not relief (2)). However, if relief (2) is to be claimed, relief (1) must be claimed first. Losses not relieved under (1) and (2) are automatically carried forward to next AP. Relief (3) can be wholly or partly claimed (so QCDs are still relieved). If loss is not fully relieved in next AP, the excess is automatically carried forward and the process repeated in the next AP and so on until fully relieved.

Cessation of trade

- The 12 month carry back period in (2) above is extended to 36 months where the trading loss arose in the 12 months prior to the cessation of trade
- Qualifying charitable donations are unrelieved

The choice between reliefs

- **How quickly relief obtained:** current period and carry back loss reliefs quicker than carry forward loss relief, so generally preferable
- Extent to which relief for qualifying charitable donations lost

Non-trading losses

Capital losses

Capital losses can only be set against capital gains in current or future APs. They must be set against the first available gains.

Property business income

Property business losses automatically set against total profits of current AP as far as possible. Excess carried forward, claim (wholly or partly) against total income in next AP.

22: Groups

Topic List

Group relief

Chargeable gains group

When presented with a group question in the exam always establish the percentage holding at each level and the effective interest of the holding company in each subsidiary. These figures will determine the reliefs available.

Group relief allows the losses of one group company to be set against the taxable total profits of another, either in current AP (current period group relief) or future APs (carry forward group relief).

Group relief group

For a group relief group to exist, one company must have a 75% effective interest in the other, or there must be a third company which has a 75% effective interest in both.

Losses available to surrender

Current period group relief
Trading losses
Excess property business losses
Excess qualifying charitable donations

Carry forward group relief
Trading losses
Property business losses

■————— ■ Capital losses cannot be group relieved.

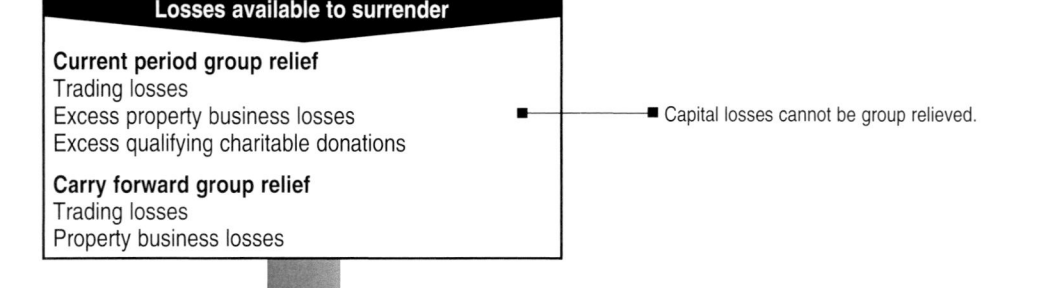

Group relief is given before relief for any amounts brought back from later periods.

Claim for group relief

A claim for group relief is normally made on the claimant company's tax return. It is ineffective unless notice of consent is also given by the surrendering company.

Corresponding accounting periods

If accounting periods do not coincide, the profits and losses must be time-apportioned. Only the profits and losses of the period of overlap may be matched up.

Available profits

Profits available to absorb group relief are total profits less qualifying charitable donations and current and brought forward losses.

Surrendering company can only surrender carried forward losses that it cannot deduct from its own total profits for the current period.

Chargeable gains group

A chargeable gains group starts with the top company (which must be included). It carries on down while there is a 75% holding at each level and the effective interest of the top company is over 50%.

No gain/loss arises when an asset is transferred within a chargeable gains group.

Two members of a chargeable gains group can elect to transfer gains/losses between them.

Rollover relief

All members of a chargeable gains group may be treated as a single unit for the purpose of rollover relief.

23: Self-assessment and payment of tax by companies

Topic List

Returns

Payment of tax

In this chapter we look at both the administration of corporation tax (CT) and when that tax must be paid. This is a key exam topic. It might be examined in Section A or as part of a question in Sections B or C.

Returns

A company must normally file its CT return by the due filing date which is the later of:

- 12 months after the end of the period to which the return relates
- 3 months after a notice requiring the return was issued

Compliance checks

Notice to check a return must be given by 12 months after

- The actual filing date if filed on or before due filing date
- The 31 January, 30 April, 31 July or 31 October next following the actual filing date if filed late

Records must generally be kept for six years from the end of the accounting period concerned.

Late filing of Return

- Initial fixed penalty is £100 rising to £200 if the return is more than 3 months late.
- Fixed penalties rise to £500 and £1,000 if the return for each of the 2 preceding periods was also late.
- If the return was between 6 and 12 months late there is an additional tax geared penalty of 10% of the tax unpaid 6 months after the filing date.
- If the return is over 12 months late the tax geared penalty is 20% of the tax unpaid 6 months after the filing date.

Common penalty regime applies for errors on return/late notification of chargeability

Due dates

Company whose profits exceed profits threshold (adjusted for related 51% group companies). Profits are taxable total profits plus dividends received from companies other than related 51% group companies.

- 'Large' companies must pay their anticipated CT liability in quarterly instalments.
- Other companies must pay their CT liability 9 months and 1 day after the end of the AP.

Quarterly instalments

- For a 12 month AP instalments are due in:
    - Months 7 and 10 in the period
    - Months 1 and 4 in the following period
- For an AP less than 12 months instalments are due in:
    - Month 7 of the period
    - Then at three monthly intervals
    - Final payment in month 4 of next period
    - Amount of instalment is $3 \times CT/n$ where n is length of AP and CT is amount due in instalments
- Instalments are due on 14th day of the month.

Interest on overdue tax runs from the due date. Overpaid tax earns interest. Interest received and interest paid are dealt with as credits and debits on a non-trading loan relationship.

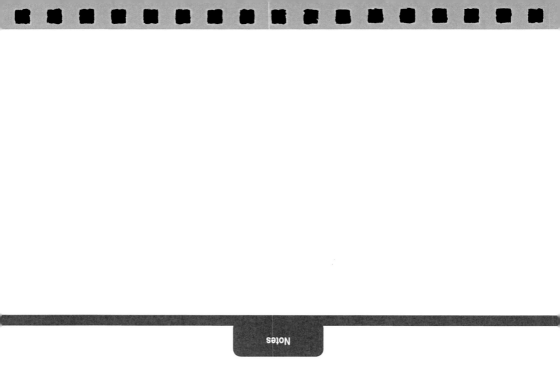

Notes

24: An introduction to VAT

Topic List

Scope of VAT

Taxable and exempt supplies

Registration

Accounting and administration

Valuation of supplies

Deduction of input tax

VAT is a tax with many detailed rules.

VAT may be examined in Section A, in Section B or in a 10 mark question in Section C.

VAT is a tax on revenue/turnover, not on profits. It is imposed at each stage in a chain of sales, in such a way that the burden falls on the final consumer.

VAT applies to **taxable supplies** of goods or services made in the UK by a **taxable person** in the course of a business.

A taxable supply is a supply of goods or services made in the UK other than an exempt supply.

A taxable person is a person that is registered or ought to be registered.

Supplies

A taxable supply is standard rated, reduced-rated, or zero-rated.

An exempt supply is not chargeable to VAT.

Gift of goods

Normally a supply at cost but business gifts are not supplies if:

- The cost to the donor is £50 or less, or
- The gift is a sample (unlimited numbers).

1 **Zero-rated supplies**

Taxable at 0%
Can recover input VAT
Eg food, books and newspapers

2 **Reduced-rated supplies**

Taxable at 5%
Can recover input VAT
Eg fuel for domestic use

3 **Exempt supplies**

Not taxable
Cannot recover input VAT
Eg insurance, education and health services

4 **Standard-rated supplies**

Taxable at 20%
Can recover input VAT
All supplies which are not zero-rated,
reduced-rated or exempt

Compulsory registration

Must register if:

1 The value of taxable supplies exceeds the registration limit in any past period of up to 12 calendar months; or

2 There are reasonable grounds for believing that the value of taxable supplies will exceed the registration limit in the next 30 days.

Notification required within 30 days of the end of the 12 month period. **Registration** takes effect from the end of the month following the 12 month period.

Notification required by the end of the 30 day period. **Registration** takes effect from the beginning of that period.

Voluntary registration

Advantages

☑ Input VAT can be reclaimed
☑ The impression of a substantial business is given

Disadvantages

☒ Increased administration
☒ Penalties if VAT/return is late
☒ Increased cost for non-registered customers

The registration limit is currently £85,000. (This limit will be given to you in the exam.)

Exam focus

The examiner may set VAT questions requiring advice to new traders (should they register, etc).

Voluntary deregistration

Can deregister voluntarily if the value of taxable supplies in the following one year period will not exceed £83,000.

VAT is due on all inventory and capital assets on which input VAT was claimed.

■ **EXCEPTIONS**

1 If VAT does not exceed £1,000 it need not be paid.

2 VAT is not due if the business is sold as a going concern to another taxable person.

Pre-registration input VAT

Reclaimable VAT is:

1 VAT on goods bought in the four years prior to registration and still held at the date of registration

2 VAT on services supplied in the six months before registration

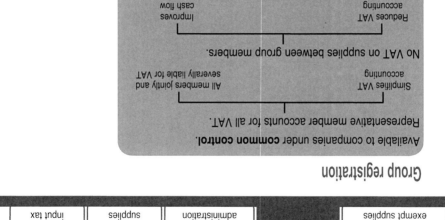

Group registration

Available to companies under **common control**.

Representative member accounts for all VAT.

Simplifies VAT accounting	All members jointly and severally liable for VAT

No VAT on supplies between group members.

Reduces VAT accounting	Improves cash flow

Any company can be **EXCLUDED** from group.

Consider excluding companies making zero-rated supplies.

Scope of VAT | Taxable and exempt supplies | **Registration** | Accounting and administration | Valuation of supplies | Deduction of input tax

VAT period

A trader accounts for VAT for each **VAT period**. Periods are normally 3 months long, but they may last for 1 month or 12 months. A VAT return is completed for each period.

Most VAT returns must be filed electronically within 1 month and 7 days of the end of the period.

Substantial traders

If a trader does not make monthly returns, and the total VAT liability over 12 months to the end of a VAT period exceeds £2,300,000, they must make payments on account of each quarter's VAT liability during the quarter.

Tax point

Each supply is treated as taking place on the **tax point**.

Basic tax point

Date on which goods removed/made available to customer.

Actual tax point

| Date invoice issued or payment made if before basic tax point | Alternatively, the invoice date, if invoice issued within 14 days after basic tax point |

Administration

- Local VAT offices carry out general administration, advise taxable persons and check that the law is being properly applied.
- If HMRC are not satisfied with the figures supplied by a trader, they can issue assessments for the VAT which they believe to be due.
- Most decisions by HMRC can be appealed against. Appeals are heard by Tax Tribunal.

Value of supply

The value of a supply is the VAT-exclusive price.

Value + VAT = consideration

The VAT proportion of the consideration is the 'VAT fraction'

$$\frac{20}{120} = \frac{1}{6}$$

Example

If total consideration is £240, the VAT proportion is:

$$£40\left(240 \times \frac{1}{6}\right)$$

Discounts

Where a discount is offered for prompt payment, VAT is chargeable on the actual amount paid.

Non-deductible VAT

VAT on motor cars not wholly used for business purposes
VAT on business entertaining (except overseas customers)
VAT on domestic accommodation for directors
VAT on non-business items

Fuel

Based on CO_2 emissions ■

VAT on:

- Fuel used for business purposes: fully deductible
- Fuel used for **private purposes**: fully deductible but account for output VAT based on actual cost of fuel or a set scale figure ■

Where cost of fuel used for private purposes is not fully reimbursed to business

Impairment losses (Bad debt relief)

- Claim within four years and six months ■
- Must be over six months old ■
- Must be written off in creditor's accounts
- Attribute payments on account in chronological order

From when payment is due ■

25: Further aspects of VAT

Topic List

VAT invoices and records

Penalties

Overseas aspects

Special schemes

For exam purposes, it is again important that you learn the detailed rules covered in this chapter.

Invoices: required details

- Name, address and VAT no of supplier
- Name and address of customer
- Invoice no, date of issue and tax point
- Details of type of supply and the goods/services supplied
- For each supply: the quantity, the unit price, VAT rate and the VAT exclusive amount
- The rate of any cash discount
- The total invoice price excl. VAT (with separate totals for zero rated and exempt supplies)
- Each VAT rate and the total VAT

Less detailed invoices may be issued where the invoice is for up to £250 (incl VAT).

Records

VAT records must be kept for six years.

Records must be kept up to date and in a way which allows:

- The calculations of VAT due
- Officers of HMRC to check the figures on VAT returns

VAT invoices are not required for payments of up to £25 (including VAT) which are for telephone calls or car park fees or made through cash operated machines.

Default surcharge

First late return/payment commences **surcharge period,** then:

Default involving late payment of VAT in the surcharge period	Surcharge as a percentage of the VAT outstanding at the due date
First	2%
Second	5%
Third	10%
Fourth and over	15%

2% and 5% surcharges are not normally demanded unless the amount due would be at least £400. For the 10% or 15% surcharges a minimum of £30 is payable.

Every time there is a default, the surcharge period is extended to the anniversary of the end of the default period.

Errors

Common penalty regime applies for errors on returns

Errors not exceeding greater of:

- £10,000 (net error); or
- 1% × net VAT turnover for return period (max £50,000)

May be corrected on the next return. Other errors to be notified in writing, eg letter.

Penalties for error may be imposed in both cases.

Interest on unpaid VAT

Interest is charged on VAT which was or could have been assessed. It runs from when the VAT should have been paid to when it is paid. This period cannot exceed three years.

Outside the EU – goods

Imports of goods from outside the EU are subject to VAT at the same rate as on a supply within the UK.

Exports of goods to outside the EU are zero-rated.

Tax point earlier of:

- 15th of month following acquisition month
- Invoice date

Inside the EU – goods

When a taxable person supplies goods to a customer in another EU country, the supply is zero rated if the customer is VAT registered.

When goods are supplied to a registered trader in the UK from within the EU, output VAT payable and input VAT claimed by UK registered trader.

Services supplied by UK trader

Export of services by UK registered trader to business customer outside UK – outside scope of UK VAT.

Services supplied to UK business customer

Services supplied to business customer in UK from within EU treated as supplied in UK. Output VAT payable and input VAT claimed by UK registered trader.

Tax point earlier of time of service:

- Completed
- Paid for

Annual accounting scheme

- Annual taxable turnover must not exceed £1,350,000 (excl. VAT)
- Annual VAT return
- Traders normally have to make interim payments on account of their VAT liability during the year by direct debits

Advantages	**Disadvantages**
☑ Only one VAT return each year so fewer occasions to trigger a default surcharge	☒ Need to monitor future taxable supplies to ensure turnover limit not exceeded
☑ Ability to manage cash flow more accurately	☒ Timing of payments have less correlation to turnover (and hence cash received)
☑ No need for quarterly calculations for input tax recovery	☒ Payments based on previous year's turnover may not reflect current year turnover

Cash accounting scheme

- Account for VAT on basis cash paid/received
- Annual taxable turnover must not exceed £1,350,000 (excl VAT)
- To join, all VAT returns/payments must be up to date (or arrangements have been made to pay outstanding VAT by instalments)

Flat rate scheme

- Optional scheme for business with tax exclusive taxable turnover up to £150,000
- Must leave if VAT inclusive taxable supplies exceed £230,000
- Flat rate of VAT applies to total tax inclusive turnover ∎
- Normal VAT invoice issued to VAT registered customers

- The flat rate percentage to use will be given to you in your exam.

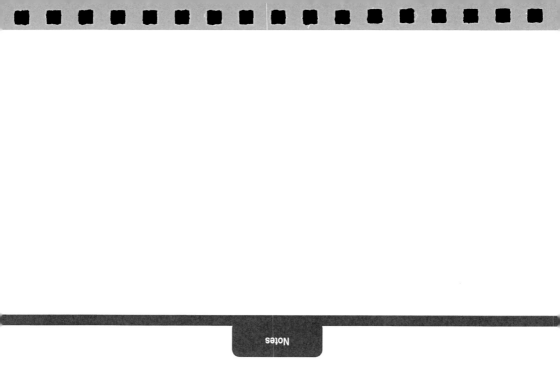

Notes

Notes

Notes

Notes

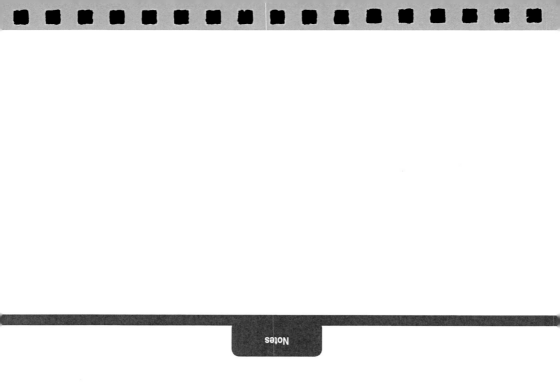

Notes

Notes

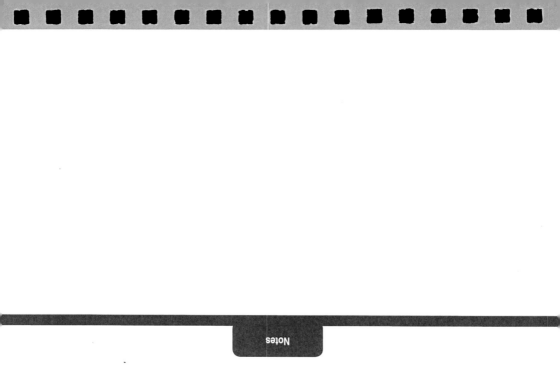

Notes